THE SALES PROFESSIONAL

This new series is designed for all sa
to get to the top of their profession.
or looking to accelerate your career, the titles in this series will
help you:

- Improve your selling skills
- Understand sales and marketing techniques
- Increase your knowledge and expertise
- Boost your self-confidence and career prospects.

Every title is:

- Packed with sensible advice
- Full of action guidelines
- Refreshingly free of gimmicks and jargon
- Written by experts.

The first three titles available are:

First Division Selling
One Foot on the Management Ladder
Prospecting for Customers

Forthcoming titles are:

Successful Large Account Management
How to Overcome Objections
The Art of Telephone Selling
How to Speak with Conviction

To find out more about *The Sales Professional's Library*, please contact:

Kogan Page, 120 Pentonville Road, London N1 9JN
Tel: 071-278 0433 Fax: 071-837 6348

ONE FOOT ON THE MANAGEMENT LADDER

ROBERT VICAR

KOGAN PAGE

First published in 1993

The masculine pronoun has been used throughout this book. This stems from a desire to avoid ugly and cumbersome language, and no discrimination, prejudice or bias is intended.

Apart from any fair dealing for the purposes of research or private study, or criticism or review, as permitted under the Copyright, Designs and Patents Act, 1988, this publication may only be reproduced, stored or transmitted, in any form or by any means, with the prior permission in writing of the publishers, or in the case of reprographic reproduction in accordance with the terms of licences issued by the Copyright Licensing Agency. Enquiries concerning reproduction outside those terms should be sent to the publishers at the undermentioned address:

Kogan Page Limited
120 Pentonville Road
London N1 9JN

© Robert Vicar, 1993

British Library Cataloguing in Publication Data
A CIP record for this book is available from the British Library.

ISBN 0 749 1192 9

Typeset by BookEns Limited, Baldock, Herts.
Printed in England by Clays Ltd, St Ives plc.

Contents

The Author		6
Preface		7
Acknowledgements		9
1	Salesman or Sales Manager?	11
2	The Role of the Marketing Manager	19
3	Finding the Right Personnel	29
4	Interviewing your Potential Candidates	37
5	Setting the Sales Objectives	49
6	Using the Right Sales Control System	57
7	Effective Communication	67
8	The Art of Delegation	77
9	Hold Meetings and Sales Conferences for the Right Reasons	85
10	Developing the Skills of your Personnel	97
11	Motivating the Sales Force	105
12	Efficient Use of Advertising and Exhibitions	115
13	Accurate Forecasting of Sales Figures	125
14	The Skill of Leading from the Front	133

The Author

Robert Vicar was born in Surrey and moved to Manchester in 1942. He was educated at Stonyhurst College in Lancashire, from where he joined the Royal Canadian Air Force, qualifying as an aircrew navigator.

He commenced his selling career in the construction industry, initially being responsible for the sale of capital engineering equipment. His total business experience has been with marketing and direct selling, both in the UK and overseas, some 20 years being spent with an associate company of Taylor Woodrow Limited, where he served in the capacity of sales manager and later as sales director.

For most of his life he has also been directly involved in the recruitment and training of the sales force under his control, and has extensive experience both in direct selling and in sales management. The guidance given in this latest book, *One Foot on the Management Ladder*, is based on that experience and the realisation that there are many ways of improving the basic skills we are born with.

Apart from his work as an author, he now operates his own company, selling specifically to the construction industry, a market which he still regards as one of the hardest training grounds for any new salesman.

Preface

‘ *We are all living in the gutter, but some of us are looking at the stars.* ’

Oscar Wilde, 1891

This is not a manual to teach you how to be a salesman. There are many books to teach you that skill, but I would hope that if you are now on the management ladder, you already will have that knowledge under your belt. As a new sales manager, what you will need to learn is a new skill based on a different set of demands and producing different results from those that have been required from you in the past. As a salesman, you were given the product that you had to sell and you will have had little influence on the nature, or even the price, of that product. You will also not have been concerned with the relationship between the cost of that product and the selling price, your performance being judged more on turnover than on profit.

What you are now being asked to do requires, among other things, a totally new concept of your job. You can, if you wish, continue to be the super salesman, and sadly many companies encourage this approach, believing that your sales talents should be used in the same way as before. Companies that operate in this way would have been better not to have promoted you in the first place as, trying to do both jobs, you will have little time to carry out the new responsibility that your company has given you.

At one time, the sales manager was very often the top salesman handling the major accounts and was judged in a very similar way to the salesmen under his control. However, as the importance of the sales operation developed, the job began to take in the costing of that operation and the balancing of that cost against the revenue that the sales manager was able to produce. His job broadened again when he became involved in the marketing plan, and so was able to influence the type of product offered and to ensure that his salesmen were selling a product that people wanted to buy.

The modern sales manager must now acquire all these new skills and in doing so he must also ensure that he is able to delegate the actual selling operation to others whose sole brief is the placing of the company's products in front of the market. Because he *is* a manager, his job must also be to pass on his own selling skills and motivate others to use those skills as effectively as he once did himself.

This book will direct you into converting the talents that you have as a salesman, and to looking at the sales operation from a new perspective. You will *still* have as your main concern the achievements of your salesforce, but if, as a manager, you counter bad selling in the field by taking over the customer yourself, you will be following the easy way out and not doing the job you are being paid for. Being a super salesman will only see you a very short way down the management road. You now have a new set of rules. This book will tell you what they are and how to match up to them.

Robert Vicar, 1993

Acknowledgements

Acknowledgement must be made to all those, both famous and also less well known, whose apt words have occasionally been quoted in the text and chapter headings of this book. My only wish is that I had thought of them first myself.

Many of the quotations have been taken from various anthologies and I should like to acknowledge the assistance of the compilers of the following collections whose work made the finding of appropriate quotations somewhat easier.

Quotations for our Time, compiled by Dr Laurence J Peter and published by Souvenir Press Limited, London WC1B 3PA.

The Oxford Dictionary of Modern Quotations, edited by Tony Augarde. Quotation used by kind permission of Oxford University Press, Walton Street, Oxford OX2 6DP.

The Bloomsbury Thematic Dictionary of Quotations, compiled by the Bloomsbury Publishing Co., London 1V 5DE.

A Treasury of Business Quotations, compiled by Michael C Thomsett and published by St James Press, London W1P 9FA.

Also my acknowledgements as follows:

To Cindy Adams quoted in Chapter One.

To Al Ries and Jack Trout quoted in Chapter Two.

To the Archbishop of Canterbury quoted in Chapter Two.

To Peter Drucker quoted in Chapters Two and Eleven.

To Henry Ford quoted in Chapter Three.

To Robert Half quoted in Chapter Four.

To Oscar Hammerstein quoted in Chapter Five.

To William Feather quoted in Chapter Six.

To Dean Acheson quoted in Chapter Seven.

To Leo Calvin Rosten quoted in Chapter Seven.

To George Bernard Shaw quoted in Chapter Seven.

To Dr Laurence J Peter quoted in Chapters Eight and Nine.

To Robert Quillen quoted in Chapter Nine.

To Will Durant quoted in Chapter Ten.

To Viscount Montgomery of Alamein quoted in Chapter Eleven.

To Stephen Leacock quoted in Chapter Twelve.

To Donald H McGannon quoted in Chapter Fourteen.

1

Salesman or sales manager?

'Success has made failures of many men.'   Cindy Adams

SALES MANAGEMENT: A NEW PERSPECTIVE

It is the job of good management to create the opportunities that others will be directed to follow. The classic description of a sales manager is simply to 'manage' and this means ensuring that opportunities, once they are known, are followed up and acted on as effectively as possible. Your new job is achieving sales, not by your own direct efforts, but through others and, indeed, if you choose to do the actual selling yourself, you are failing to do the job for which you are paid. Both the analysis of the sales opportunities and the insistence that they are pursued, are two demands which someone who has been a salesman up to now has not previously had to handle.

You are no longer a film actor but a film director, and while it may irk you to sit in the chair and direct someone whose acting ability may not be as good as your own, *that* is what you now have to do. Accept that the job you now have as a sales manager is in addition to what you were doing before and, assuming your new appointment was needed in the first place, you will fail because you will not have time to do both jobs properly, and it may even be worth questioning the thinking behind the new appointment. Where you previously decided a course of action and saw it through, you will now have to learn to delegate. If those others to whom you delegate are unskilled, you will need to train them. If those others are incompetent, you may well have to fire them. In the American vernacular, you are in a different ball-game.

A MANAGER'S ATTRIBUTES

Look at any advertisement for a new manager and you will swiftly see what is being called for:

- you must be able to motivate;
- you must be able to select the right people to work for you;
- you must be able to communicate with your subordinates;
- you must be able to control what you have set in motion;
- you must have imagination and enthusiasm;
- you must be able to plan.

All these will be new skills as, apart from enthusiasm, your selling career as a salesman has not really called for any qualities other than the ability to sell a product which your company has decided is right for the market. A salesman's sole interest is in his own success, financial or whatever, while that of a manager must inevitably be in the success of others and how they contribute to the overall success of the enterprise he is running.

Visualise, if you will, the bad managers for whom you have worked and consider why you thought them to be bad. Without question, they will have been lacking some of the above features and almost certainly one of the first two.

The skills you will now develop will be different from any you have had up to now. If you find that the title of sales manager offers little more than the opportunity of a better name on your calling card and does not, at the very least, require you to consider changing either the product you are selling or the way it is being sold, then you probably have not really been given the job of a manager at all.

NEW APPROACHES TO A NEW ROLE

You need to look at what you are now being asked to do and appreciate how the changed specification of your job is going to alter the way you handle it. A manager who relies on using his original skills, but with more authority than before, will not get far without the new human approach which he must now cultivate to accompany them.

- First of all, it is assumed that you have probably been a good salesman and that you have gained your promotion because of that success. You still need that sales knowledge and expertise, but will equally certainly not have the time or the ability to use it in the way that you have in the past.

- Secondly, you must recognise that a sales manager has a different set of problems from almost any other manager in business. Whereas a manager controlling, for example, administrative or works personnel, generally has his subordinates working relatively close to him, the sales manager will always have an immediate problem of supervision simply because his sales force is operating in the field, distant from him and not always in close communication.

- 'Management to survive' used to be the popular phrase to describe the kind of organisation that you now need to create to meet the crises which arise from falling sales or from recession. It means that every factor which affects your company needs to be considered against all other such factors. If any one of them stands in the way of increased or more profitable turnover then it needs to be evaluated and, if necessary, changed. I say 'if necessary', because sometimes, in the light of the overall picture, for example shortage of available cash, some obvious problems need to be accepted until more important problems are solved. Up to now you will have had little influence to change the many factors which you probably knew about but were unable to alter. It will now be part of your everyday job to recognize these factors and to adjust your management policies to deal with them.

- You will need to become skilful in selecting the right personnel to carry out your requirements. If you consider the real reason why in your private life you deal with one company or supplier rather than another, it will almost certainly be the people in the successful business who are responsible for retaining your loyalty. If you, in your business, can either employ people who will project a similar high level of service or can train your existing staff to do so, you will probably have less need to lean on special pricing and discounting to keep the customers you have and also attract new ones.

- Right from the start you need to sit down and analyse the job you have been given, both from the angle of what your company wants and what you believe your customers want. An enlightened management may well have given you a job description, but rarely will it cover all eventualities. Generally you will have been left some degree of freedom to determine where your responsibilities lie and how much authority you can secure. Any new appointment should have been the subject of a proper discussion by those appointing you, and they will have needed to decide what they were expecting you to achieve and how you were to be judged (and rewarded) for doing it.

Unfortunately, human nature being what it is, there will always be grey areas where lines of authority are not as clear as they might be, and it is in the early days of any appointment that those lines can be made more definitive. If senior management have not worked out such a schedule of your responsibilities, then you will need to do it yourself, so that, after a few weeks in your new position, you can discuss the interpretation of your job to check how it matches with that of the directors who appointed you. It is always essential to have clearly defined objectives, if only to know, at the end of it all, whether you have achieved them or not.

Remember, in the days when you were a salesman, you were normally judged by a relatively simple evaluation of your sales figures, something over which you had every control. You will now be judged by many other factors, most of them linked with the appointment, handling and motivation of your people, and your results must now come from the efforts and achievement of others. Make sure you are given the authority to control the performance of those others.

MANAGEMENT STYLE

When you take over as manager, particularly if your new subordinates were your previous colleagues, you have one basic decision which will determine the kind of staff relationship you will have in the future. That decision is the style of management you are going to adopt. This is not so much the detail of your administration or even the mechanics of your job, but is essentially the attitude of mind with which you approach your new position. Take the easy-going, friendly way and the strong employees will take advantage of you; take the heavy-handed way and you will get compliance but little co-operation.

Unfortunately, for this most important of your early decisions, there are no real rules and certainly no rigid guidelines you can fall back on, but, without doubt, you can be certain that the average salesman would prefer to see firm leadership as the proper alternative to the over-familiar approach, and is not looking for a soft touch which will make his life easier. You can be sure, however, especially when you have been promoted over colleagues, that there will be attempts by those colleagues to retain as much of the previous relationship as possible. You will consequently need to maintain your distance in the early stages while you are determining the style of management which is most appropriate. If in the first instance, as a new manager, you clearly indicate which way you intend to assert your authority, you can always soften your approach later when you have the workforce behind you, but, doing it the other way round, implying that little has changed and that you are still just one of the salesmen, and you will find the option of later changing course and direction will not be available to you.

Management style is probably the greatest difference between the good and the bad sales manager, and by and large there are fewer easy-going managers than hard-hitting ones. It is possible to be both easy going and good, but the odds against it are much greater and you had better be sure that you can fight those odds before you make your decision in that direction.

Think hard of the successful business tycoons you know of, because you have just put a foot on the same ladder. Analyse for yourself how many of them are probably regarded by their workforce as hard taskmasters. To be successful, you will need to be regarded in the same light. Your salesmen will be aware that a consortium of ideas is unlikely to work unless one man is prepared to make the important decisions and they will accept an intelligent decision as something they were happy not to have had to make themselves. Your job is now not just to obey the rules, but also to make them and, having made them, develop yourself into the kind of manager who is prepared to make sensible exceptions to them when the occasion demands.

The reasons for forgoing the over-familiar approach are many, but the most obvious comes from the concept of the job that you now have been given. Your role is now concerned with working with subordinates who may well have a very different view of the job you are all doing. You are also working closely with the directors and policy-makers of the company, and your decisions must now reflect and represent an authority which at times you may not agree with yourself. Your subordinates will not have that split loyalty and if you aim in your new position to be 'one of the boys', you will find it very much more difficult to implement decisions with which they, and maybe you also, disagree.

DECISIONS, DECISIONS . . .

The differences in your new position will also become apparent when you find you have a number of different problems presented to you at the same time and you need to allocate priorities. In your old job as a salesman, you had one specific job with no element of management decision and little responsibility other than ensuring your customers both bought your product and were satisfied when they had done so. There were certainly decisions concerning which customers you called on and in which direction you aimed your car in the morning, but those decisions were all related to selling and normally the answer to them was reasonably self-evident.

In your management position, the job is no longer clearly defined and, while your main responsibility will still be the turnover and profit figures of those salesmen in your control, you will now have a separate and linked responsibility for finance, for recruiting and training, and for staff control. If you are to develop the necessary skills, you must make an allocation of time which managers are often not prepared to give. That is why many managers fall back on the selling skills that they know and ignore their new responsibilities in favour of continuing to develop the old ones. It is essential to remember that your job as sales manager means that you no longer have the time to be a salesman too.

To ensure that you *do* have time for you new responsibilities, you will need to recognise the importance of planning your time more effectively than you have in the past. You will need to plan your day for the important matters and delegate the responsibilities for which you do not have the time. This delegation must necessarily include passing over to others the responsibility for your own cherished customers and, while you may feel they will not be so effectively handled that way, it will now be your job to recruit, or train, personnel who can do the job as competently as you once did yourself.

These are some of the changes that you are going to meet and they will have little to do with the basic principles of selling. What they will have to do with this is your ability to influence those who now work for you. That is the skill that you must now develop and is the skill that you have not needed until now.

CHECKLIST

- You are no longer a salesman. Management is a full-time job.
- Recognize the qualities that a manager must have.
- Understand the many factors which can affect your sales targets.
- Select the right personnel to whom you are able to delegate.
- Ensure you know your limits and what authority you have been given.
- Plan your time to make space for your new responsibilities.

2

The role of the marketing manager

> *'If you want to go out and do battle with your competitors, it is helpful to know where to go.'*
> Al Ries and Jack Trout, *Marketing Warfare*

WHAT IS MARKETING?

It should be unnecessary to stress the point, but so many publications refer to *marketing* as if it is some kind of *selling* that it is essential that the proper distinction is made. My dictionary lists the word as 'Buying or selling in a market', which does little to offer a real definition. Indeed, many books written to define marketing have eventually surrounded the subject with such mystique that the average layman, still failing to know what it really is, continues to refer to marketing as a generic term for the whole business of selling.

Marketing is not selling. It comes a long way before that and involves the basic research which will decide the product that you offer, the price you will offer it at and the people you will offer it to. It is simply because most of this information will probably come from the active selling field that the jobs of marketing and selling are inevitably linked. In a large company the jobs themselves may well be separated, but they certainly cannot be isolated from each other. In addition, as a newly appointed sales manager, you may possibly be your own marketing manager, and it is as well at this early stage to know what this division of your job is actually about.

To quote Peter Drucker, 'business has only two functions, marketing and innovation'. Marketing, as opposed to selling, is making sure that what you are selling, and the way you are selling it, is what the customer actually wants now and is going to want in the future. The salesman who walks from door to door selling an undesirable piece of kitchen equipment, is a salesman pure and simple. If he is an effective salesman, he may even be successful, but he is being successful in spite of the fact that *the original marketing of his product was faulty* and what he is selling is not really what his customer needs. Marketing aims to make sure that particular hurdle is removed from the course.

MARKETING IN CONTEXT

The marketing operation is concerned solely with establishing, in advance, that there exist people who, once contacted, are reasonable prospects to become customers for a product which meets a particular specification. Marketing is not concerned with finding those customers, except in a somewhat general way, or even working to make sales to them – that is the job of the selling division – but it is concerned with doing all the work *from the aspect of the product*. It involves making or offering something that people want, making it so that it is available when people want it and, probably above all, making it at a price that the customer is prepared to pay. If the marketing man gets any of these criteria wrong, he has made it difficult for the salesman who later tries to sell the product to the customer.

The market, of course, can be directed or encouraged to lean towards your product or service and a demand can be created where none previously existed. That is why advertising also comes under the control of marketing, for here the responsibility is to increase the demand before the salesman, or the retail shop, or whatever, offers it to the customer.

In some cases, the salesman never really appears in the final act of selling at all. In the field of fast moving consumer goods (FMCG), for example, you as a customer will buy a new brand of cereal because other influences such as advertising, or possibly an elaborate display in your supermarket, have encouraged you to do so. At this level, marketing almost takes over the job of selling.

In most businesses it will be a combination of the marketing and selling operations which actually secure the business, the advertising because it either has encouraged the customer to seek more information (or has weakened his resistance to the salesman who calls) and the salesman himself who converts that need into a firm commitment to buy. If the marketing work has been correctly done and the right product is being offered (and that means competitively offered), the job of the salesman will obviously be a great deal easier. People are influenced by good advertising, whether they are prepared to admit it or not. Quoting a past Archbishop of Canterbury, 'I do not read advertisements, I would spend all my life buying things.' Consciously or unconsciously, advertisements *are* read.

PRINCIPLES OF MARKETING

So, how does the marketing man work? Why should his results be any better than the old-fashioned salesman who sold what he was told to by a management whose only gauge of the market was whether they were selling enough of their product to satisfy the targets they had set themselves?

Marketing people are essentially statisticians who endeavour to separate the available customers into categories so that they not only know who they are selling to but also which are the most likely groups to accept their product. The old joke about dividing the potential customers into groups 'broken down by age and sex' (aren't we all?) is the traditional starting point and, within practical limits, the more divisions you have, the more likely you are to be able to find the best market for your product. I say 'practical' because you must restrict that breakdown so that you have categories which are also easily usable in your advertising, your retailing or whatever. Those classifications will change as the markets change and you would be foolish if you did not monitor those changes also.

It is vital to make what you are offering as close as possible to what your customers want or consider reasonable to buy and you will have more subsequent success when you later try to sell it. Try to make the customers adjust too violently to your way of thinking rather than their own and you have made your selling job more difficult.

In 1987, it was easy to sell a Porsche to a yuppie. What you were offering matched both what he wanted and what he could afford. By 1990, the appeal of the same car to the same person, at the same price, had altered, simply because the income of that same yuppie was dramatically reduced and no amount of good selling could alter that fact. Good marketing, however, *might* have avoided the problem of cars remaining on the shelf, either by anticipating the drop in demand and making fewer units, or by directing the product at a different market where the problem, at that time, did not exist. Maybe the car could not have been made cheaper to meet the changed market, but at least the professional marketing man should, and hopefully did, look at that possibility also.

The real marketing people, and that means those who rely as much (or more) on marketing as on selling, for instance those concerned with FMCGs, will have accurate classifications of as many customers as they can find, where those customers live, how old they are etc., and the advertising of that company will be targeted in magazines or promotions to attack just those markets. That is why circularised junk mail will arrive on *your* doorstep and not on that of your neighbour, simply because on some distant mailing list, you are in one category (maybe because you have children) and he is in a different one (possibly because he is retired). This kind of categorisation is, of course, valuable to such a company and only you can tell from your own marketing research whether it is equally valuable to you. But certainly, before you start selling to your customers, you will need, one way or another, to know who those customers are and how you can get access to them.

TELLING THE CUSTOMER ABOUT THE PRODUCT

After having determined your product and then having decided who your customers are, you will next need to know how best to present your case. An advertisement in the *Daily Telegraph* will not reach the same customers as would an advertisement in the *Sun*, and if your research shows that more of your customers actually read the second paper, then obviously that is where you will need to place your advertisement. In addition, the layout of the advertisement in each paper would sensibly not be the same (although regrettably, for reasons of convenience, it very often is.) Customers do look at presentation in different ways and it is vital to offer your information in a way which the customer finds acceptable. Empathy in advertising is as important as empathy in selling and your customers must react easily to what you have to say. If your customers find difficulty in absorbing the written word, then maybe pictures, or even a cartoon strip, will get the message across more effectively.

Advertising is probably the easiest sales ploy to insert into your sales programme and almost certainly, except in the FMCG market, the most difficult to evaluate. I remember being told many years ago, by the marketing manager of a large washing powder manufacturer, that they were able to take a television advertising spot on a Monday and by the Friday knew how successful it had been. In most businesses you do not have that reaction, and apart from return-card mailshots and newspaper coupon returns (which only tell part of the story anyway), you have little guide on whether a particular advertisement in a particular publication is effective or not. Remember the often quoted remark by a company sales director that 'he knew half of his advertising really worked but he was unable to find out which half'. You, unfortunately, will have the same problem.

Advertising is, however, such an essential part of marketing that it is vital you get it right. It is rarely a matter of how much you spend but very much more in what manner and direction you spend it, how you use your empathy to ensure your advertising is acceptable and how you use your skill to place your advertising where it is going to be seen by your potential buyers, whether that is in the *Financial Times* or in the subway under Hyde Park Corner, or both.

PLAN YOUR MARKETING

Always, in preparing your marketing plans for the future, you will need to look at the many factors which will influence your decisions.

- Will the competition upstage you with something so new that overnight your own product will become obsolete?

- Is the economic climate likely to kill, or even kindle, your business? You may not be able to influence the economic climate at all but you must certainly be able to plan for any changes you can see ahead and move with them as they arrive.

- Are there any new markets where you are already close enough to take advantage of their potential and so easily branch out into areas where you have not operated until now?

- The market itself, in the context of the customers you have available, is constantly changing, either by age or by numbers. This will affect your ability to sell to certain classes of people and may well open up your chances to sell to others. If factors such as changes in the birthrate, for example, overtake you before you realise they are there, you will have expensive catching up to do to handle those changes. Anticipate.

MATCH YOUR PRODUCT TO YOUR CUSTOMERS

In your marketing function, your object is to ensure that the sales team, whom I am assuming you also control, are provided with a series of product features which are acceptable to your potential customers, and that all your marketing will be angled to ensure that they are correct.

- Initially you must, of course, make sure that the product is right for the market and that it is basically what people want to buy. It is one of the easiest errors to make in selling to assume that because you think it is good, that everyone else in the market will think the same. The road to bankruptcy is paved with memorials to those who tried to change the requirements and demands of the buying public.

- Your product or service must be set up at a price which your customers are prepared to buy. If it is so good that it prices itself out of the market, then you will obviously need to

The role of the marketing manager 25

redesign it to make sure that it seems good value and is financially acceptable to those who will consider it. The actual value or pricing of your product can only be determined by what your customers will pay for it. There is no other criterion and if what it costs you as a supplier is more than the figure that the customer will pay, then, if you are unable, by planning and economies, to alter that basic cost, you will be wasting your time pressing for a sales price which is unacceptable.

- You must look at your potential customers and ensure that these are the ones you are targeting. If the product does not sell because you are telling the wrong people, then you must look elsewhere for your market. If it does not sell because you have wrongly judged the demand for it, then you will need to offer an alternative product which does have an immediate market. However, it is not impossible to misread why your market is failing and you may well in hindsight find you have discontinued a viable product simply because you made the wrong decision on why it did not sell.

- You must inevitably keep a regular check on the methods you are using to get your product on the market and not rely on the fact that because you have always marketed that way, it is necessarily the right way to continue doing so. Sometimes a direct sales operation can be effectively replaced by a system of agents or distributors or even by franchisees, any of whom might be able to locate and deal with your customers better (and more cheaply), than you are doing yourself.

- You must also look at the competition with a somewhat broader definition than is customary. The majority of companies will view competition as those companies or products that are similar to their own, but vary either in technical content or price. For the marketing person this is too narrow an interpretation since in the marketing context we must regard competition as any product or service which is being considered by the customer as an alternative to our own. It is easy, for example, in the investment world, to consider competition in terms of, say, national savings or building societies, since both have the same final object of security, but it is not too far fetched a concept to consider competition also as the local pub or the betting shop because both will be options for the customer as possible alternatives where he might spend his money.

Many of the decisions which will be taken as a result of your evaluation will be partly marketing and partly selling, but they certainly do not fall outside these two disciplines and it is to be hoped that the two policies will come under your control. It will be equally important for you to decide that the price you determine, even if it is producing an acceptable profit for your company, is not set at a level so low that the customer rejects the product or service simply because it appears too attractive an offer to be seriously considered. Estimates for all sorts of products are often rejected because the customer feels that his proper security has not been safeguarded in your price. It is as well to remember that, for all products, there is a band within which the customer expects a price to fall. Offer it above or below that price and you have a problem on your hands in convincing your customer to buy against the fixed ideas he already has in his mind.

CHECKLIST

- Real marketing is not selling.
- Sell the right product. Are you offering what the market wants?
- Know your potential customers and where to find them.
- Advertising can often be the way to create the market before you start the sale.
- Constantly look at the way your market can change or be changed.
- Marketing means constantly monitoring the competition, knowing what they are planning and, if necessary, producing it before they do.

3

Finding the right personnel

'It is all one to me if a man comes from Sing-Sing or Harvard. We hire a man, not his history.'

Henry Ford

ROUND PEGS, ROUND HOLES

Recruitment of staff is, of course, the most important part of ensuring that the people you employ are either matched to the position you are filling or, equally important, can be matched by subsequent training. There are inevitably pitfalls in the selection of anything, whether it be a new salesman or a new television set, but many of these can be avoided if you have spent a little time beforehand deciding what you are actually expecting to achieve.

If, in the first instance, you get your requirement specification wrong, however good you are at the selection end, you will almost certainly not select what you really need. The first part of the employment process must therefore be the outline of what you want from any new employee. You must know what others in your company will expect and, while these views will be subjective and may clash with your own, you will nevertheless have to reach some sort of compromise with your colleagues so that once your man has been appointed, he is at least capable of handling the work that others may be anticipating from him. As a consequence, when you prepare the job description which will eventually form part of a new contract of employment, it is essential that all those managers who have an interest in a new employee get together to make their own contributions to that job description.

THE JOB SPECIFICATION IS VITAL

Initially, if it is a new position, the job title will need to be determined, and if it is a replacement you might need to consider whether the previous job title now accurately defines a job whose demands might have changed. The actual moment of recruitment is probably the only time when you can easily rewrite the demands of that job or even eliminate the position altogether. The straight replacement of one employee with another similar one can often be a guaranteed way of perpetuating a problem which you have failed to recognise in the first place.

There may well be responsibilities to be added and certain existing responsibilities may well be better placed with other staff. Companies *do* change both in their size and their style of management, and, while it is easier to continue the way something has always been done, it is sometimes more effective to change it. You will not get a better time than the moment when you are replacing one manager or salesman with another. In the same way you can review the hierarchy of who reports to whom and ensure that potential problem areas which may have become evident in the past can be avoided in the future.

SALARY MATTERS – AND QUALIFICATIONS

Matters such as salary and remuneration may well be relatively rigid in a large organisation and a round-table discussion will produce little except jealousy or disappointment, depending which side of the fence you are on. I would suggest that while you will need to know from your company directors where the payment scale is likely to be pitched, the actual figures will be one decision you will be taking on your own. The two words in an advertisement, 'salary negotiable', do not really mean that, as your own budget will tell you what you intend to pay; the phrase generally indicates that the offered salary will not be published in the media and consequently to all your other staff.

At the same time as you create the job description, you must also know how qualified your recruit will need to be to cope with it. In addition, your colleagues who are also involved in the decision will need to have a say to ensure that the company is not saddled with someone who is either too qualified or too incapable of doing the job. With a list of essential characteristics at your disposal, you will gradually be creating a filter which, long before the interview stage, can be used to separate the possibles from the impossibles.

You have now created, or revised, the description of the job you are seeking to fill. You have outlined the kind of person, possibly the age, certainly the qualifications and experience, and probably the existing track record of your potential candidate and you know what you are looking for. You now need to consider the methods you will employ to find such a person in the marketplace.

It may, of course, be that you have a potential candidate already in your employment. If you have, fine, but make sure that in your enthusiasm to employ him, you do not omit all the planning I have suggested above. Your candidate may well meet all the criteria of the original job, but a swift reappointment can lose you all the advantages of reassessing your requirements. Make that reappointment and you might well find that a better or a differently qualified person could carry out that job better, or indeed the job could be more effectively split up among personnel who are already on your staff.

RECRUITMENT OPTIONS

To ensure that you have the most suitable candidates, you have many options at your disposal.

Consultants

You can hand over the whole selection process to a team of specialist consultants who will, for what you may consider an exorbitant sum, look at the personnel registered in their own records, advertise if necessary and eventually arrive with a short-list of possible candidates for you to interview. The problem here is that an agency does not know your own personal requirements and someone with whom you might have been able to have worked easily does not, for one reason or another, get through the first agency interview and you consequently never get to see him. You have not been personally involved from the outset (except for the job description that you supply to the agency), and this, in my view, presents the biggest disadvantage to using a third party to do the sifting for you.

Against that you have the availability of personnel trained and experienced in interviewing, and you may even be lucky enough to choose an agency which already has a suitable candidate on its books. In addition, you cannot ignore the fact that the method should certainly save you time, since, generally speaking, an agency will be able to short-list a set of candidates somewhat more swiftly than you might be able to do yourself.

Headhunting

There are other methods of recruitment in the same mould and, depending on the level of employee you are seeking, the use of headhunting must be considered as a possible option. The method does work, but it is an expensive way of securing what you hope is the best person in the business and has the obvious disadvantage that if someone can be bought from your competitors, then later on he can be equally easily bought from yourselves. However, that is the problem with all good employees. In any case, your close knowledge of your industry should already be providing you with the names of those top salesmen you would like to encourage to your side and it is arguable that you are failing if you need to employ a third party to do your searching for you.

Existing employees

You will necessarily look within your own organisation, but you will need to be somewhat careful to make sure that you do not take an existing employee down the interview road and then fail at the end to give him the position. You may then find that you are looking for two replacement employees rather than one. It should go without saying that at a very early stage you should have enough information on your own existing employees or those in other divisions in your company, to make sure that the ones you are talking to have a reasonable chance of matching up with the position that you are offering.

Personal recommendations

Anyone in the recruitment business will tell you that a very high percentage of jobs are filled without any advertising being done at all. Because of this, you will certainly need to have a permanent ear to the ground to ensure that you are aware of successful employees of your competitors who are dissatisfied with their present positions.

Headhunters, as mentioned above, make their money by supplying such information, but it is not too difficult in a relatively closed industry to become aware of such potential employees and to ensure that they also are aware that you have a suitable vacancy available. Always talk to managers of other companies in your area, even discuss your requirements with your bank manager, since he does, after all, talk to many other people during his working day and it is probably in his own interests as much as yours that you get it right. You will also have the advantage that by using personal references you will have some prior knowledge of the sales capabilities of your potential candidate.

Buried treasure

One neglected area is the value of letters which have been previously written by applicants to your company in the past and which, simply because there were no vacancies at the time, have been filed away 'for future reference and we will write to you if anything suitable should arise at a later date'. This is poppycock! I know of few companies who actually have a proper retrieval system for such applications and the lack of it probably means that a great deal of time and effort is spent on finding new potential employees when the information was in the company files all the time, and could have been retrieved with minimal effort. Leaving aside everything else, even if that employee is now satisfied with his present position and no longer wishes to move, he may well know of someone of quality who does and will pass the word on to him.

Other organisations

There are, of course, other organisations who can help you, such as job centres and the professional register, but do not be surprised if they do not produce what you are looking for. The high-flier salesman will usually make it his own business to promote his availability and will not rely on others to do it for him.

ADVERTISE WITH CARE

Failing all else, you will need to advertise, either in the national press or in the technical press of your own industry. This is a high cost activity and guidelines from your own financial director may well be necessary to make sure that you have a budget which is acceptable to your company. However, it is not too difficult to quantify the savings and potential profit you will gain by getting your employee on stream one month earlier than you might otherwise have done.

Remember that replacement of staff is expensive and is one very good reason for taking steps to ensure that you need to do it as rarely as possible. Your problem, of course, particularly if the job is an attractive one, is the sheer numbers of applications that you will have to sort through. Advertising being what it is, the resulting applications will probably have a lower general standard and a higher number of rejects than those acquired by other methods. As an amateur recruitment officer, you might find it difficult to select a reasonably practical short-list on which to work.

Consequently, when you advertise, remember that you are paying good money for the space you are taking and that your sole object is to get as many usable replies as possible. This does not mean as many replies as possible, because that is easy, but as many replies that have a chance of being taken to the next stage of an interview. This means looking closely at what you say and where you say it so that you encourage the possible and discourage the time-wasters. Too often the approach of 'just run the same advertisement again' is taken as the easy way of restarting a recruitment process with little regard as to whether that particular advertisement produced the right result last time. Before you book your space, ask yourself the following questions and check your answers to see whether there might be options which would produce better results.

- Is the publication you are considering the most widely read in the industry and is it also most likely to be read by those you are trying to contact?

- Does the quality and style of your advertisement reflect the quality of your company and the job that you are offering?

- Have you described the person you want to employ in a way so that the reader identifies himself with your description? If you know that you will be demanding certain technical qualifications, have you said so?

- Have you described the job so that when a candidate comes to you for an interview, he is already aware of what he will be expected to do? If you hear at interview, 'That's not really the job I want', then your time (and his also) will have been wasted.

DISCARDING UNSUITABLE APPLICANTS

Somewhere between the finding of the right personnel and the interviewing of them will be the sieve which thins out the possibles from the unlikely, and makes the job of initial interviewing a great deal easier. You will, particularly if your job is an attractive one, or if you are in a period of high unemployment, have applications from many people who are obviously unsuitable but who write almost in desperation for jobs for which they are neither qualified or matched. The next chapter will deal with the actual interviewing of those who are suitable, but it is vital before that stage to ensure that you have deleted all those who have no chance of making it to the final selection.

Application forms at this early stage will make it easier to remove those impossible applicants so that you can compare like with like and concentrate your efforts on those who have a chance. To see everyone who chooses to reply to your advertisement (on the basis that otherwise you might just miss a possible) is a waste of your time and is moreover an indication that your job description was not tight enough to discourage the undesirables from writing in the first place. You will have enough to do at the next stage of interviewing and short-listing at this early point will ensure that you have the time to do it.

CHECKLIST

- When considering the appointment of new staff, the job description is the only starting point.
- List out the qualifications and personal standards that you require.
- First look for new staff within your own organisation.
- Decide whether to delegate the selection to an agency or whether to do it yourself.
- If you take advertising space, make that investment with care. Indifferent advertising will bring indifferent applications.

4

Interviewing your potential candidates

'The best person you interview isn't necessarily the best person for the job.'
Robert Half

At this point, when you are close to planning the interviews, you need to compare the relative merits of those applicants who, on the basis of their applications, appear to be generally suitable for the job. It is now that you will appreciate the value of a systematic approach to framing the job description, the recruitment advertising (if any) and the application form. If that approach was undisciplined, you will be looking at a wide and varied range of applicants who seem to have little in common, and you will find it very difficult to draw any useful comparisons between candidates or to select a group for interviews.

COMPARING POTENTIAL INTERVIEWEES

Now begins the process of elimination. If, for instance, you believe that an age of 35 is really what you are looking for, you will need to eliminate those who totally miss that criterion, but you must also be prepared in your comparisons to quantify those who come close enough to be considered. You might be prepared to accept 5 years either side, but a candidate of over 60 or under 21 should miss your bracket altogether. Unless you have rigid guidelines, you will find yourself interviewing all the applicants, each of whom has a valid claim to be considered, probably different in each case, but many of whom who also have a disadvantage which would, if you thought about it, prevent them being considered at all. If you have already decided in your job description that a PhD is vital, then don't waste your time (and their's) interviewing those who have not got one. You may indeed miss out on someone who could have done the job, but in that case you will have been implementing a faulty job description.

Leaving all else aside, it will make your interviewing process almost impossible if you do not know what you are looking for. You can, of course, work on the principle that if you throw enough darts at the dartboard, one at least will hit the treble 20, but because that system occasionally *does* appear to work is no justification for using it.

In Chapter 3, I advised you to make early use of an application form and there is no doubt that a well-constructed form helps to standardise the initial information that you get on each candidate. This *must* be designed to present the information that you require in a concise and easily read standard, and it is not for nothing that the boxes for filling in on the form are sometimes as small as they are. If the information needs to be expanded, it can be done at interview, the application form itself being designed to ensure that only the comparative information that you require is initially available. If you have the complete life story of each applicant in front of you at the beginning you will have great difficulty in extracting the specific information that is needed.

Your interviews will then be based on a number of prospects who, on paper anyway, match up to the job description that you and your colleagues have prepared. From then on the decision becomes less clear cut and more subjective. If you are carrying out all the interviews yourself, the situation is somewhat simplified, but if, in either the first, second or third interviews you have chosen to have assistance from your colleagues, your problems may well begin to start, as, unless you all actually do agree, the decision that you make may well not be unanimous. My own view is that the fewer managers involved in the actual decision making, the better. I believe that personnel selection is one of the main responsibilities of management that should be taken by one individual. You are, of course, as liable to make a mistake as anyone else, but then so are the others on your interview panel and a vote of 2:1 for one candidate is by no means proof that that candidate is the best choice. If it is a subjective decision, and all decisions of this type must be, it is probably better that it is your own.

THE INTERVIEW. A GENERAL APPROACH

The interview itself must always be controlled so that both the potential employee and the employer are relaxed enough to understand what the other is offering. I have never believed that trick situations (to gauge reaction) are even marginally useful, although many companies still use them to create a 'what if' position. There are potential candidates who can deal with staged situations in a professional way and yet, when employed, will not show the same initiative and resource. By creating a 'test' atmosphere rather than that generated by a discussion, you will tend to lose the co-operation that you need to make sure that you are both making the right decision.

It cannot be emphasised too often that the interviewing has to be two-way to be effective. Very often a candidate who has all the qualifications and is of the quality that is required, does not go any further with his application because there has been a failure by the interviewer at the first interview to sell the job which is on offer. There are now too few good people about for the employer to take the same autocratic line as he might have taken in the past. Fail to sell the good qualities of your company in the same way as you expect the candidate to sell his own good qualities and you will not get the people you actually want to employ.

The essential aim of your interview must be first to give as much information as possible both about you and your company, and secondly to secure as much information as possible regarding your candidate. Without doubt, the best way to do this is to ensure that your candidate is relaxed and that the initial impressions you have given him, even before the interview starts, are favourable, so that he does not arrive antagonistic and unwilling to provide the information you need. Remember, there *will* be detail that he would rather you did *not* know and your job is made harder if you are working with only half the facts. Below will be found a few guidelines on getting the co-operation of your candidate.

Interview confirmation

When an appointment has been made, always confirm it and, if necessary, give guidance as to how to reach the location where you will meet. The candidate may already know the meeting place, but your own professionalism will be emphasised to him, possibly for the first time.

Make him feel expected

Make sure that the staff who will meet the candidate, including the receptionist, are expecting him. They also have a part to play in convincing your candidate that your company is the one he wants to work for. If all you are aiming to do is employ people who need a job, you will finish up with all those employees that no one else wants.

Start on time

Always commence your meeting at the time you arranged. Not five minutes later. As with your selling approach, punctuality does matter, and your object is to convince the candidate of your professionalism. Interviewing is not a one-way business and any employer who thinks that he holds all the cards is fooling himself or will wind up employing the wrong person. Always remember that the last applicant you really want is the one who desperately needs your job and you have to work at it to secure the high flier who has other alternatives available.

QUESTIONS AND ANSWERS

Your interview will, of course, demand answers to a series of questions, none of which you will be able to ask with any certainty of getting a straight answer.

- Is your man reliable and persistent in following through whatever he takes on? Ask him and he'll say – Yes.
- Has he other interests which might clash with what you will demand of him. Has his spouse or partner a business which takes up some of his own time? Has he an overactive private

life? Has he an alcohol problem? Ask him any of these things and he will tell you – No.

- Will the job be too much for his level of competence and experience? Ask him and he will certainly say – NO.

- Is he aiming for the salary that you are offering? Ask him this and he will swiftly say – Yes (even if he really wants more and will move on as soon as he finds it elsewhere).

- Is his claimed knowledge of the industry as good as he says it is? Here it will probably help you if you are specific in discussing contacts in companies whose set up and personnel you are familiar with. It will then not be too difficult to know first of all whether he has the contacts he claims and also at what level he is accustomed to dealing with a company.

All the information which really answers these questions is vital to you and will need to be secured in a way which will give you more reliable answers than the ones the candidate may want to give you. But be certain that if you do not get the valid answers, you will certainly find out later, as possibly his previous employer did.

INTERVIEW FROM STRENGTH, WITH CONTROL

In any employer/candidate interview, the employee will, if he wants the job at all, be the one who is apprehensive and nervous. As an employer you will probably be over-eager to fill the position you have advertised, but really, that apart, the cards are stacked in your favour. You are not looking for a job, you are in your own environment and, one hopes, you have a good choice of candidates. The interviewee has none of these advantages and it is essential that the interviewer, being the one person who stands in the way of what the candidate wants, is seen as a person to whom the candidate can talk. For that reason it must certainly be your first job as an interviewer to establish a rapport which will make the interview more useful to both parties.

When you ask questions, you will still need to maintain that rapport and that means achieving a balance between interrogation and seeking information. Remember that they are not the same

Encourage the candidate to talk. What you are doing at interview is identical to what you have always done as a salesman, which means listening more than talking and directing the conversation in the way that you want it to go. But, as in your sales style, losing control of the discussion is the swiftest way to exhausting all the time that you have for the meeting and securing nothing from it. Remember that your candidate is probably no fool either and if he can get the job at the right salary without revealing the odd skeleton that he has in the cupboard, then you may well have bought problems for the future.

It is important to recognise that selection of staff is a simple matter of your knowing in detail the job you are offering, analysing the interviewee and deciding whether one matches the other. The interviewee has the same job to do and, except in the short term, has little to gain by taking on a job for which he is obviously unsuited. To discover any problem, possibly before he does, it is vital that you use your 'empathy' and that you look at the job as much from the candidate's angle as from your own and so gauge whether his eagerness to accept is based on real acceptability of the job or whether it is coloured by the fact that he has nothing else on offer.

You are aiming to find out, not just the technical qualifications of the person you are interviewing, but what kind of person the candidate really is. You must be looking for enthusiasm and commitment as much as skills, and you should always have in the back of your mind that it is probably better to employ someone with no knowledge at all but with the enthusiasm to learn, rather than the person who has all the knowledge but not the commitment to putting it into practice. Particularly in selling you will be looking for people with perseverance who will keep going when business is bad or non-existent. A frequent change of jobs may well indicate a lack of stamina in seeing something through and will need to be analysed before you accept the candidate's reasons on why he has been unable to stay in one place for too long.

Always remember that you must look closely at past performance as a guide to the future. It may well be that there have been reasons, and good ones, why your candidate has failed in the past, but one who has made a mess of his career, or his life, over the past three years, is probably going to do the same in the next three. Certainly there is always the person who is resolved to get it right next time, and this will be most persuasively put while he is in front of you at interview, but you are taking an unwarranted risk if you stake your money on him doing just that. Your job is to limit that risk and leave the 'give him another chance' approach to someone else. Tough, but then that is what the manager's job is all about.

You must always, however, make certain that the decision to employ is not hurried simply because you believe that you cannot give it any more time or because you have no one else to consider. If your candidate does not satisfy all the criteria you have set for the job, don't employ him. A realisation that you made the wrong decision in the first place will be expensive for your company, will take time before you can do anything about it and you will still be left with the same recruitment problem that you had in the first place.

For all the advice I have given above, the recruiting process is still far from being infallible. You can still select the wrong person from a short-list of six and you can continue to be surprised at the superlative performance of someone who was appointed by chance simply because there was no one else available. If you are able to minimise the chances of making an error you will have done well, but no cast-iron selection method is yet available. All business is inevitably moving in a direction where computer analysis of character and written qualifications are taken more seriously than selection by intuition and experience. You would be foolish to ignore the first two, but do not forget that the last method is still probably the most important of the lot.

INTERVIEW TECHNIQUES

At interview, try to quantify all the impressions you are getting, awarding marks on a scale which is related to the importance of that particular characteristic in your selection process. After a morning's interviewing, it is easy to emerge with a whole bundle of different opinions and pictures of the candidates, all of whom have impressed in one way or another, but unless you are able to sort them out into some sort of scale to judge one against another, you will find it impossible to select your best option. Because people are so different and because the specific features you are looking for will be so different, you must bring your applicants down to some common level so that you can balance the qualities of one candidate against the qualities of another. This is even more important when your interviews are being conducted over a few days and you have other matters in between to distract your attention.

Very early on in your discussion, you must find out with some accuracy whether the candidate still has a job he is expecting to keep, whether he is actually under notice or whether he is anticipating redundancy. This information will always be somewhat jealously guarded and may not even be easily found out by contacting his present employer. There *are* often private arrangements between an employee and his present company which tend to cloud the reasons for going and they can colour, not only the reasons for leaving, but also the kind of reference you get when you ask for it prior to his actual appointment. A failure to get hold of this information from the start will often lose you the advantage of knowing why the applicant approached you in the first place.

REFERENCES ARE IMPORTANT

At the end of the appointment process you will have made some decision to employ one or other of the candidates and will then need to follow up the information that you have acquired to check whether it is valid or not. People *do* claim qualifications which they do not have and, while such qualifications may become less important, the further back they are in a candidate's career, nevertheless you might believe it necessary to check again if it turns out that some of the information you have been given is less than the truth.

The following up of references is equally important and, while it is unlikely that you have been given the names of personal contacts who will contradict any of the information you already have, some of the former employers, if approached, might be more forthcoming about your candidate's previous performance. You will, of course, when talking to these earlier employers, not be aware what personal relationship they had, or still have, with the candidate and for that reason, it is better not to rely too heavily on what you are told. In addition, it may well have been part of the deal when they parted company for the departing employee to be given a 'good reference', regardless of whether he deserved one or not. This can often be a way of smoothing out the hassle which can accompany the ending of a period of employment and, if you are trusting the answers that you get, you might just find yourself buying the same problem that his earlier employer was trying to get rid of.

It is as well when you check any references never to ask for an opinion as this will rarely give you the real answer that you require. The previous manager, after all, will probably have known the candidate in his personal life and will not be looking to create an enemy that he did not have before. Moreover, if the employee was a problem, he no longer is one and the past employer can see little personal advantage in hindering your candidate from getting a job somewhere else. Your easiest approach is always to ask the former employer to verify whatever individual facts you want to know and you will find that you will get a straight, short answer rather than an opinion which might be based on something other than the truth. You will, after all, have been presented with various claims from your applicant on whether or not he can do the job and it should not be too difficult to rephrase these as questions which are easily confirmed or otherwise. Probably the best question of all to ask a previous employer is 'Would you re-employ him?' The straight 'yes' or 'no' is possibly the most reliable answer you will get.

It is, however, worth realising that you should not be too dismissive of someone who is quoted as having one or two weaknesses. The reaction of different people to weaknesses is subjective and what may seem major to someone else may well be minor to yourself. We all have our weaknesses and unless they are so damning as to make employment prohibitive, we should merely balance them against the good qualities which are also on offer. Bear in mind anyway that a candidate with no apparent weaknesses has probably still got them. You just haven't found out what they are.

Finally, when you make your decision and create a letter of appointment, make sure that it is a letter that you would wish to receive yourself, and that it would make you enthusiastic and excited about your new job. If you do not think this is important, dig out the letter of appointment for your present job and read it through, and see whether it really has the selling capacity that it should. Whether it has or not, make sure that your own letters in the future do something more than list out the bare facts of what has been offered.

KEEP IN CONTACT WITH NEW EMPLOYEES

Probably the last piece of advice is that the engagement of a new employee certainly does not stop when you both sign the contract. You will then have a great deal to do in the first few weeks of employment to ensure that your new employee is satisfied with what he has done with his career and that he is not immediately believing that he would have been better off somewhere else. Ask your new employee some two or three weeks after he has been appointed whether what he has now found out about the job matches up with what he expected. If not, why not and is there any way it can be altered so that everything can be set back on course? In this initial period, any new employee will be looking for guidance, while after that period he may be more resistant to accepting a change in his own approach. Remember that a new employee, who leaves after his first month with you, leaves after a month of advertising and a month of interviewing, and his departure will be followed by at least a further two months before you find someone else. It is worth a little effort to ensure that four months are not wasted, particularly if your chosen candidate was also the right person for the job.

You should, at the very least, set up a system which either you or a nominated subordinate must follow to monitor those first few important weeks to ensure that the time spent in placing your candidate in his new position is not wasted. The rules are simple and are all based on using your empathy to see the new employee's position from his point of view.

- If the new employee is young and inexperienced, make sure that someone specific is detailed to guide him in the mechanics of the office. For instance, I once worked in a new office for a whole week before I discovered that they had a canteen.

Sometimes a youngster will be reluctant to ask about something which everyone else takes for granted.

- The job that has been given must be explained in detail so that the new employee is aware of what is expected of him, and where his responsibilities start and stop. He will need a job description which is comprehensive and readable. The job must be properly explained and that includes early introductions to the people he will be working with in departments other than his own.

- A senior member of staff must explain the thinking of the company, not the detail (which will be the responsibility of his colleagues), but the principles on which the company is run and how those principles are put into practice. I worked for many years with Taylor Woodrow Limited and great emphasis was always placed on the thinking of the founder, now Lord Taylor, on how each individual member of the group should be treated. Loyalty is the pay-back, and in such a company it can always be recognised by the number of long-serving employees among its members.

- Remember the enthusiasm with which you employed your new candidate, and his own enthusiasm when he accepted the job, and keep that momentum going in the first month or so when every new day will bring problems he has not met previously. He will be looking for guidance and, if he does not get it, you can be assured he will rapidly join the ranks of those who work in a company but form no real part of it.

CHECKLIST

- Before you interview, set out your essential standards.
- When you appoint, make the decision your own, not that of a panel.
- All interviewing is two-way. You stand to gain as much as the candidate does.
- Quantify all your interviews to one standard so that you can compare one candidate with another.
- Your job must also be to discover problems your candidate may not want you to know.
- References are not reliable. You will only be given the good ones.
- Your responsibility for a new employee does not stop with his appointment. Retain his enthusiasm in those first few weeks.

5

Setting the sales objectives

'If you don't have a dream, how are you going to have a dream come true?'
                                            Rodgers and Hammerstein

THE OPTIONS FOR SETTING SALES TARGETS

Once the marketing function has identified a product which has a market available to you, and the company has manufactured or prepared the product, you will then have the job of setting your own sales targets and your plans to achieve them. As a sales manager you have various options available.

Sell more of the same to the same people

You can manufacture or offer more of what you are offering already simply because your figures tell you that there is still wide scope to expand with your existing product into your existing markets. This will, of course, lead you into the areas of employing more salesmen, improving the salesmen that you already have, employing more administrative staff to handle your existing enquiries more effectively or even making use of more advertising to get the message out to those potential customers who have not heard of you.

Sell more of the same product to new markets

You can continue to manufacture or offer your existing products or services, but you may need to look for new markets outside those where you have been dealing up to now. There may well be other areas where you have not looked and you will need to wear your marketing hat to analyse whether areas you have not exploited up to now could offer a potential you have not really considered. Once markets at home have been exhausted, you may need to look at the possibility of foreign markets. This again will demand a hard marketing operation to distinguish markets with real profit potential from those that might produce turnover, but will be unprofitable in doing so.

Sell something different

You can alter the base of your company and either manufacture or offer something else to fill a gap which obsolescence of your existing offer is leaving. In the domestic appliance market, for example, there is a constant programme to develop equipment to handle work which previous generations were happy to do manually. In the financial world, changes in taxation can suddenly make unacceptable an investment which for years has been attractive and you will be persuaded into changing what you do simply to meet the demands of the customer. The new development may be a product which is similar to the one it replaces, but may even involve total diversification into something new. A takeover of an existing company often leads you into a new and unfamiliar field, and is a superb opportunity to use available expertise to handle something which you would not have considered up to that time. An example which in the end failed to have the success which it might have had, was the takeover of estate agencies by insurance giants in the late 1980s, which resulted in a great emphasis being placed by the estate agents on the financial services being offered by the insurance groups who had bought their way into the system, giving them direct access to a market they had not previously had.

POLICY AND RESOURCES FOR THE FUTURE

At this stage of your planning you initially have to decide the policy for the future, using the marketing knowledge which has either been presented to or acquired by you. The implementation of that policy will be something different, but right at this early stage you will need to be looking at the resources which you have and liaising with other managers who will tell you whether you have the skills available to carry out what you plan to do. Do you have the personnel to whom you can delegate the additional work involved or, alternatively, have you the training facilities to retrain extra personnel should you need them? You will also need to know whether your production team or your administrative staff will be able to work to the timescale that you have in mind. These will all be factors and influences where, as sales manager, you will need others, not necessarily your subordinates, to report back to you on whether you have included impractical considerations in your forward planning.

First, in any operation, you need to know what your own or your company's objectives really are. This sounds simple, but more errors are made because a company does not know which way it wants to go than are made by companies who fail to achieve what they are setting out to do. As Peter Drucker says, 'Management by objectives works if you know the objectives. Ninety per cent of the time you don't.' As an initial reaction, your company may say that the object is to sell as many widgets, or houses, or wheelbarrows, as possible. This is certainly the easy way out in that it gives no real targets and, passed down the line, it will mean eventually that the same ambition will be passed to the salesmen in the field. As a result, without a real target, no one has anything specific to strive for and no one really has any indication whether he has reached a goal or not.

The problem in creating a situation like this, and many companies do just that, is not that those companies do not know their ambitions. Very often they balance their spending and investment for the future on what they have earned in the past rather than the reverse, which is to know in advance what their realistic targets are and to base their spending on achieving that figure. In the end, if spending is exceeded or if targets are not reached, the result is the same, but it is extremely difficult to plan any operation unless the sales or income potential is calculated at the beginning and the other figures are developed from that.

Your sales figures must, of course, come from your marketing operation. You must know, from that operation, whether what you are offering has a potential market at all and, from your own research, how much of that market you can secure. If you are already selling the product and have ambitions to expand, you need to be aware of the percentage increase that might be considered realistic. 'Increase sales by 50 per cent' is all very fine, but without the marketing proof that it is even remotely achievable, you will be asking for trouble if you allocate a 50 per cent increase in expenses in order to achieve it. Always plan to choose objectives the logical way, which means selecting ones which can be measured. Set valid objectives in numbers, in percentages and in dates so that you can then be just as specific when those objectives are either achieved or missed.

You may, then, decide through your marketing division, or indeed with your own marketing hat on, that a 10 per cent increase in your sales is possible, either with new markets or alternatively by taking existing markets from your competitors, not forgetting in the latter case that they may well be adopting the same approach. If you are convinced that what you are doing is realistic, it is not then too difficult, either from your production team if that is the type of business you are in, or your financial colleagues if that is more appropriate, to work out exactly what would be the likely additional expenditure to your budget and what additional income might be produced. Remember that additional business might well produce more gross profit but in doing so could well demand additional expenditure in divisions and areas other than your own.

You then have a gross income figure and your company policy will tell you how much of that you can actually spend to achieve it. (There is, after all, little use in earning an extra £500,000 if it costs you £600,000 to secure it.) The resultant net profit figure will be the basis you can use for additional expenditure in motivating your existing sales force, employing new personnel or even opening new branch offices. Do all this the other way round by developing your sales operation in order to see what extra business you can achieve and you will do little except provide yourself with a shock when you find that your income does not meet your additional expenditure. Unbelievable though it is, this is the way that many businesses expand themselves, often eventually into bankruptcy.

SETTING TARGETS FOR SALESMEN. AGREEMENT IS VITAL

Let us assume you have five salesmen who each produce an annual turnover figure of £700,000. You will gain little by sending them all a memo saying next year that figure will be £800,000 offering either incentives (or threats) when they reach (or do not reach) the new target. It can be done this way and very often is, but unless those salesmen believe that what you are suggesting is achievable, you will merely demoralise them by asking them to attain the unattainable (or at the very least what they think is unattainable). This is when the technique of management by objectives can be extremely valuable.

MANAGEMENT BY OBJECTIVES

Management by objectives really means management by agreement and essentially implies that your salesman has agreed with you that what you are doing is valid, possible and practical. In the reaching of that agreement, there may well have been compromise, but in principle both you and your employee have discussed his potential as a salesman, the quality of the product he is selling, the potential of the territory which he has been given and the time he has available, and you have agreed that, with all the plus and the minus factors, what you are asking him to do is reasonable. In return for his achieving it, you will agree to reward him, first by continuing to employ him (no small confidence booster in itself) and perhaps additionally with commission, or an incentive prize, or whatever it is you have decided will help him in reaching that goal.

You may believe that a discussion of this kind is in some way abrogating your own responsibilities as manager. However, doing it the other way by imposing a target without discussion, is about as reasonable as a board of directors telling a sales manager to increase sales by, say, 60 per cent without any regard or consideration as to whether it is a practical target or not. The salesman who has agreed to the targets you have discussed together will at least not be demoralised by being asked to do what he believes is the impossible.

You will by now have taken the opportunity to speak with your sales team and, in agreement with each of them, will have sales estimates from which you must judge whether you can achieve your new aims with the staff which are available to you. You will have taken some sales forecasts from your own salesmen with a pinch of salt and adjusted them accordingly, but in the end your salesmen will have accepted sales objectives which will form part of your own plan. You may now have to increase the sales force (or even find you can legitimately decrease it), but in any event you will have split up the target you have set. Individually, of course, the salesmen will have to split it up yet again among the potential customers they have in their own customer records and calling schedules.

That is really the basis for setting sales objectives, but it must be emphasised again that the increased expenditure you incur must always be planned as a result of the increased income you are aiming to secure. Spending cash on additional salesmen when a few moments' thought (plus sensible discussion with your existing salesmen) will tell you that no extra business is there, is the fastest way to put yourself out of business. The decision not to employ may well lead you back into the marketing operation again so that you can rethink your product. That way, while it may be disappointing, is better than walking over the proverbial cliff. Easy possibly in hindsight, but think how the British motor-cycle industry might still be successful today if they had looked properly at their market, as indeed the Japanese looked at that same market and been able to decide what machines to produce to meet the proper demand.

It may not always be the job of sales managers to run companies, but it is certainly their job to produce the eventual profit and the job of the marketing division to decide what the sales division is able to offer. Hopefully you are now aware of the responsibility of the job you have taken on.

CHECKLIST

- Your options for the future. Expand or diversify?
- Make use of the marketing information available to you.
- Where does your company actually want to go? If they don't know, then make sure that they, and you, develop a plan which can be effectively followed.
- Can you afford the development you have planned?
- Ensure everyone else knows the direction you are going. People will only co-operate if you have told them what the plan is.

6

Using the right sales control system

'Why do you need it on paper? Do you not trust me?'
Adolf Hitler, Munich, 1938

SALES FEEDBACK AND THE CONTROL OF SALESMEN

In any company with an outside sales force, there should be a continuous flow of information from the field, the proper use of which is vital if the sales operation and, more particularly, the marketing function, are to plan correctly and accurately for the future. It is often a feature of poorly managed companies that the system under which they work has been allowed to become casual and, as a result, information which is acquired and known in the field does not make its way back to the office where it can be profitably used. Sometimes the information is religiously supplied by the field sales force, but there is then no system laid down for analysing and using it. Either way, if you let this happen, you will be throwing away one of the strongest planning tools that you have available and also not properly monitoring the performance of your sales force in the field.

As a sales manager, you will swiftly become aware, if you do not know it already, that your salesman is the most expensive liability that you have and, if your management is ineffective, the one over which you have the least control. You can, if you wish, even quantify that liability so that you know what each call, effective or ineffective, actually costs, so that you can make your salesman aware of the responsibility he carries when he selects the customers on whom he is going to call. However, whether he knows the cost or not, it is essential that the call is used to secure either the business, which is what it is all about, or at the very least all the information that you need to extract regarding the future potential of the customer. It is then vital that this information is passed back efficiently to the sales office so that it can be used to plan the strategy for the future.

Most salesmen who do not like written reports, and that means about 99 per cent, will justify that dislike by saying that their job is to sell and that writing reports merely takes time away from that selling operation. Often even good reporting systems are not complied with and management can contribute by being unwilling to make report completion a matter of discipline since they feel that by doing so they might lose the good salesman who refuses to comply. If you, as a manager, tend to accept this view, I believe it is likely that you will be unsuccessful because you have failed to convince your field personnel of the important reasons why those reports are required. As William Feather said, 'Beware of the man who cannot be bothered with detail.'

If you have a system and fail to manage it, it will swiftly become mediocre, and the only way to ensure that it stays as good as it was when it started is to control it with a proper discipline. On the other hand, if the manager is receiving information which patently he does not require or use, and fails to delete it from the system, he has only himself to blame when his sales force reject the whole reporting system as a waste of time.

PRINCIPLES OF A CONTROL SYSTEM

First, whatever report system you develop, it must supply you, and the salesman, with the information that you and he both need for analysing performance in the field. That may sound naive and simple, but a quick look at any system, particularly one adapted from a standard form, shows that the little boxes which require completion often demand information which appears to have little relevance or value at all. If answers and information are being requested and you cannot find any reason why the request is being made, then delete that section and revamp it. You will always get co-operation from your sales force if what you are asking has an obvious reason. You will get little co-operation if no one can see reason in the system being there at all.

For instance, if detail of daily mileage is important so that you can decide if a territory is too large or if a salesman is spending too long in his car for the business he is doing, then that information must be in the report and the salesman must know why he is putting it there. However, if no one ever analyses those figures, why collect them in the first place? Early in my career, I religiously used to enter on each daily report 'Time of First Call.' No one ever told me why, except possibly that they wanted to know whether or not I was capable of getting out of bed in the morning, and certainly the time I put down bore little relation to the actual time the first call took place, so immediately the importance of the report was weakened. Other information I completed was, I know, never read, and was only inserted because it had always been done that way.

So, if necessary, rewrite the report completely so that it does provide the information that everyone wants and, in this case, consultation with the salesman, and indeed everyone else who reads the report, is important. Remember that the salesman also may need to have information recorded which he will use on his next visit. Aim to get that also on the same report form which he returns to you.

For the same reason you will need to involve your salesmen in the analysis of the sales targets that you have jointly agreed, since the failure of most reporting systems is that those who write them invariably believe, and with some justice, that no one ever reads them. If you have believed in the past that this is true of your company, then you are not alone. Systems that have cost a great deal to set up (and take a considerable time to complete in the field) are often not read in the office, partly because no one has the time and partly because the information was not needed in the first place. They are, however, often left in existence because it is felt that they produce a sales discipline of which the salesman is at least aware. If that is the best you are expecting from your sales reporting system, then the sooner you scrap it the better.

In order to set up a system which does not rapidly become

bogged down by its own sheer volume, you need first of all to know what information you are really looking for and what you can effectively use.

Identification of markets

You obviously need to know where your customers are and if there is a recognisable pattern that will guide you for your future business. It is very often the case that one salesman has found a market where another has not even bothered to look and, conversely, a new salesman may spend excess time looking at a potential market which your experience will already have told you is a waste of time. It is unlikely that one salesman will pass this kind of information to another and it is your job as a manager to ensure that guidance such as this, which has been expensively acquired, is passed on to others who can use it. While still giving your salesman all possible freedom to explore new markets, it will be the good sales manager who analyses and compares trends from one area to another, and tries to guide the sales force to look where the business is most likely to be and to direct the sales force away from areas which have proved timewasters in the past.

Geographical location of customers

You need to know the geographical locations of your customers, where they are concentrated and where you have barren areas, so that one salesman does not have so many potential customers that he cannot deal with them and another has too few to cover his operating costs. The second will probably tell you soon enough, but you are unlikely to hear from the person who has more than he can handle and is turning in record sales figures because of it. Either way, both salesmen will be working inefficiently to the detriment of your national turnover figures. The traditional territory split is often by county boundaries, or even by the allocation of cities, and either of these methods may not fairly assess what business is available in those areas. It is difficult to get your balance right but you will certainly not be able to secure an accurate assessment of your salesmen if you do not know what potential each has available to him.

Selling the range of products

You need to know whether the salesman is selling across the range or whether, because it is easier, he is concentrating on selling one product only. This is a problem because, even if he is managing to move the most profitable business, other potential business is being turned away simply because it is harder to sell. It may be that the solution is to reduce the size of the territory so that the salesman is compelled to work his area correctly, or it may be that training is required to sell a particular part of the range more effectively. It may even be that there is a case for applying an incentive to that part of the range to even out the balance. There are loss leaders in any organisation which are often required to be there to encourage business from other directions but, unless a salesman is selling across the range that you offer, he may well be achieving turnover without a balanced profit. Whatever the solution, you will not be able to work it out if you do not know the problem. It is essential that you are aware of how each salesman sells and what he sells. The facts will all be available in the invoicing records, but many companies just do not take the trouble to look at them.

The importance of customer records

Most important of all, you need to have a proper evaluation of all your customers, both those who give you business and those who do not, including a comprehensive record of all the detailed information that has been acquired. Record cards *do* get lost from company vehicles, information often goes adrift when a salesman leaves and all this expensively acquired detail is the property of your company. You risk losing the basis of your trade if you do not have on record, in the office, the same information that the salesman has in the field.

There are few salesmen who do not have their own personal file of customers and contacts which they have built up over the years. It is your job as manager to make sure that as much of this 'black book' as possible is also entered on the company files that you maintain. You will, of course, as sales manager, not necessarily collect and maintain this information yourself, but the sales office manager most certainly will and should regularly have access to it when he is presenting his assessment to you. If a customer is worth calling on, it is certainly worth recording the fact that you have called, what the result was and whether that customer has potential for the future. Given the facility of computer records, there is really no excuse for any sales-oriented company being unaware either of where their potential customers are or of who their salesmen are targeting.

TREAT INFORMATION WITH CARE

The actual use of information from the field must be interpreted sensibly, since, if unconsidered action is taken by the company on the basis of the salesmen's returns, you will begin to get facts and figures which distort the real truth. If, for example, you insist on ten calls a day, that is what you will get listed on your salesmen's report and all you have achieved are figures which are no longer reliable. I would assume that the old method of telephoning a sample batch of your customers 'to check if your man has been in there recently' is not part of your process. If it is, and you want to maintain the trust of your sales force, you need to rethink your policy.

Your main problem, as a manager, is to ensure that the information you receive is presented first in a way that it can be easily used to help you formulate your decisions, but also in a way that ensures your sales force do not regard it as the reason for their existence. The regular complaint from the field will always be that there is too much paperwork. Whatever you do, it is unlikely that you will avoid this traditional cry, but a salesman is an individual who generally works better alone than he does with others, and you will need to convince him that the closer link you are seeking between him and the sales administration is something which will benefit him as much as it will benefit the company.

You do not need to know where he is every moment of the day (even though it might help) and any attempt to get that sort of relationship will certainly end in disaster, but somehow you will need to separate those salesmen who work effectively from those who do not. I have seen sales reports which require you to state the length of time taken up with one customer and asking at what time you arrived at the next one. If you feel that from this information there are useful actions you can take, then fine, but if you do not, the information is a waste of time in the first place, and anyway, it is unlikely that what you are being told on the report has any great similarity to the truth. Why ask when all you will be told is what the salesman thinks you want to hear?

WHAT INFORMATION DO YOU REALLY WANT?

A sales department that attempts to operate without all the relevant information that it can get will have little value to the marketing operation (which needs to plan future developments), will have little value to the publicity department (which needs to plan up its current promotions) and will have little value to the sales manager (who needs to assess the performance of the field force under his control). Since you, as sales manager, take the decisions, make sure the sales team know exactly what information you need to have available and how you want it presented.

The information you do need from the field will depend largely on your product. If a business relies on how many customers the salesman actually sees, the sales manager will need details of each salesman's call rate so that he can analyse it against other salesmen with the same conditions. If your company is selling battleships, the salesman's call rate will probably be irrelevant and will tell the manager little about the way he is doing his job. If the size of the company he calls on is important, possibly because it is cheaper to service a large company than a small one and you consequently make more profit, then you will have much more interest in knowing the *type* of customer who is being called on. Without the detail of what you are looking for from the field and without that information in the report, it is unlikely that you will even begin to use your reporting system correctly.

DRAFT A REPORT FORM

Having decided, perhaps in conjunction with your colleagues, what you require from your sales system, you will need to design the layout so that it provides simply and clearly the information that you want to know. There are commercial systems on the market which cover everything from selling bridges to paperclips, but I have yet to see one that does not also demand useless information simply because it is trying to cover every eventuality and requirement that might arise. While these may be better than no report form at all, it has to be far better to take time laying out that form and the details required from it in the format which best suits your own company business.

If, for instance, demonstrations are an essential part of your selling presentation, you need to know how often these are arranged and how often they result in securing the business. The end result with one salesman may well be the same lost order, but it is essential that you know whether he fails because he cannot convert a demonstration into an order, whether he cannot sell the idea of a demonstration in the first place or whether he is demonstrating to the wrong people. With the right information at your disposal, you can at least compare one salesman with another, and establish a set of criteria against which you can judge ability and performance. You will also have the advantage that, in introducing a new system, you can tighten up the discipline regarding its use and operation.

FINAL THOUGHTS

A proper sales control system is essential if you are to know what your people are doing with their time. Many companies regard sales turnover figures as the only real criteria on whether a salesman is good or bad, but this fails to acknowledge that certain geographical areas may well have problems that others do not and that all sales conditions are rarely the same. A strong competitor, an established buying pattern, a previous record of bad service by your company, may well result in an excellent salesman battling against the odds, but turning in poorer results than average, and if you act on that turnover result by an out-of-hand dismissal of the salesman, you could well still have the problem but have removed the one possibility you had of solving it.

It is your job as a sales manager to control and remedy poor sales figures, but to do it you need to have at hand a great deal of information, sifted if you like by your sales administrator, but information designed to give you the detail that will help you in

Using the right sales control system

sorting out the good from the bad. It is your decision to decide what information you need and, particularly in a new job, it is unlikely that the system that is there already will give you what you want. If it doesn't, the sooner you scrap it and confine it to the bin with other useless statistics, the better. Leave the old system where it is and not only will you not be managing, which is what you are paid for, but you will not be getting the detail you do require, and both you and your staff will be spending a lot of time producing and analysing figures which have no practical value.

Remember that whatever information you request, you should always have at the back of your mind the possibility that the salesman who is providing it might not be as permanent as he appears. People do move on. If he leaves you, that is one problem, but if in addition he takes with him the customer details that have been so expensively acquired, you will be paying a lot of money in the future to secure the same information the second time around. This does happen, simply because the sales manager did not have the imagination to consider that a salesman might leave or even be fired (when he will be even less co-operative). Make sure that his customer information is also yours.

CHECKLIST

- Develop a sales report that is practical, then make proper use of the information on it.
- Ensure your salesmen know why a reporting system is being set up.
- When the report has been submitted, always analyse the figures with the salesman who completed it.
- Bad paperwork usually means a bad salesman.
- Always gather customer information centrally on the basis that your salesman may leave you for another company.

7

Effective communication

> *Extremists believe that communication means agreeing with them.*
>
> Leo Rosten

ASPECTS OF COMMUNICATION

Open the book for the first time at this chapter and the odds are that you will be expecting a lecture on how best to pass your instructions down to your colleagues. However, if you have already read this book from the beginning, you will probably realise that this chapter is going to be one of the most important in your path to becoming a most effective manager. It covers the whole principle of talking to your subordinates, listening to both your subordinates and your superiors, and generally controlling the whole two-way communication process, the success of which separates the good manager from the mediocre.

Communication is a natural skill which we all possess as part of the human race and yet, in virtually all incidents which occur daily in the world, the degree of success or failure in communication invariably plays a major part in the result which occurs. Two cars may collide with each other because the driver of one failed to tell the driver of the other what he was planning to do. This is a simple example possibly, but if there had been an effective way of one letting the other know that he was going to stop or start or turn or whatever, then the subsequent collision might not have occurred at all.

Communication (or the lack of it) is equally responsible for the majority of understandings which happen in our business lives. We would have far fewer problems if more attention was given to telling our staff, and our directors, why we intend to do something, what we are trying to achieve and, at the end, whether or not we have achieved it. It is often because we do none of these things that our actions are misunderstood and our decisions, which are possibly the right ones, are interpreted down the line as being ill conceived. After all, most business decisions are subjective and may well not be obviously correct, but we have less chance of convincing others that they are the best unless we take the time and trouble to sell those decisions to the people who will have to implement them.

COMMUNICATION IS A TWO-WAY PROCESS

Communication is both the passing out and the receiving of information, but if one had to choose between the two definitions, the most important would inevitably be the ability to receive information from others and to use the ideas that are offered. As employers we spend a great deal of time, for example, analysing the skills of those we intend to employ. Yet, having employed those people, we then spend far less time in using those same employee skills simply because we do not go to the trouble of discovering whether or not those employees might have an opinion, or be able to make a contribution which is possibly more valid than our own. Communicating with employees is important, partly because without it we are not properly using the ideas we have bought and also because there is little doubt that more company problems can be blamed on a failure of communication than on anything else. Ask yourself whether the following ideas form part of your everyday method of working.

Do you discuss tasks or problems?

Do you talk regularly to as many of your staff as possible about the jobs you have given them? If your personnel lack some of the qualities which their job demands, are you prepared to train them? Have you discussed with each salesman, first his objectives and secondly whether those objectives match up with his ability? Your employees in their work may have problems in which no one appears to be interested and which indeed may well eventually press them into seeking employment elsewhere. That is both expensive and a waste of talent when, by a little effort, the problems could have been opened up and solved.

Do you listen for ideas?

Do you listen to the ideas of others, who, at the very least, will have subjective views on the same query you are trying to solve? Those others might just have a better angle on the problem – maybe they have encountered it elsewhere – and might come up with a better solution than you have yourself. Ask and listen, since, all else aside, your employees will appreciate your interest in their opinion. Regularly fail to ask that opinion and you need not later complain when you are left to solve your problems on your own.

Do you discuss career development?

Do you, as a matter of policy, regularly advise your employees where their careers are going? Do you know the qualities and abilities of each salesman under your control, and do you in fact have career plans for them at all? Most employees are seeking some kind of promotion or advancement (or even change), but rarely are they told that this is even a possibility for the future. By personal communication with your staff, ensure that they are aware of the direction in which their future with the company is going. If your personnel are unaware of their future, they are easy prey to your competitors.

Do you explain policy initiatives?

Do you take time to explain changes in company policy and procedures? We need to 'buy' the loyalty of employees by ensuring that they know why changes are being made, why additional staff are being taken on, or why redundancies are being introduced. Worker participation (in the broad, not the political sense) avoids unnecessary misunderstanding of changes in an established system. A memo usually tells your staff the new rules. Proper communication tells them the reasons why the new policy was necessary. The first without the second merely encourages aggravation and breeds resentment over changes which are not understood. You may not always make your staff happy with new ideas, but you certainly stand a better chance of doing so if they understand the motives behind them.

Does each employee understand his place in the overall scheme?

What we are trying to do is not purely altruistic. We are aiming in the first place to make our operation more cost-effective by everyone having a clearer picture of the final objective so that they will become more efficient in trying to get there. In the car production line, if a worker did not know what part he was actually making and what was its importance in the end product, then he had little incentive or interest to make that part properly. Not so long ago that was exactly the case, but that philosophy has now changed, not least because the Japanese have made perfection an object in itself. They have also developed the art of communication down the line to ensure that everyone knows what he is doing and why he is doing it, not especially for the benefit of the individual worker (although he will gain by having more pride in his work), but for the benefit of the company and its effectiveness in the market.

Do you check that information is properly received?

In addition to the communication down the line, which is the kind which transfers information about changes, about policies and about achievements, it is vital that we also set up a system which feeds back reaction, ideas and even knowledge on whether the information has been received properly or not. This feedback is at one time the most useful to receive and the most difficult to encourage.

Ask yourself the following questions, and the answers may help you to assess the nature and effectiveness of your system of communication, and whether it needs to be changed.

- What am I trying to tell them?
- Do the personnel who are receiving the information really need to know it? If they don't actually need to know it, will it help if they have it passed to them?

- Which of your staff really needs to be informed and what is the best way of getting close to those particular people?
- Is the style of the information tailored to those who are to receive it? Remember we do not always have the same ability to receive and absorb facts and figures, and for the same communication, different presentations may well need to be designed for different audiences.

COMMUNICATE BY SPEAKING TO PEOPLE

To appreciate the value of analysing your own effectiveness in communication you need to accept that there are still many sales managers who believe that the remote 'instructions from a distance' approach is the only way of maintaining discipline and respect, and very often these are the ones who are the most surprised when a valued employee, who has both salary and position, leaves the company to find a different kind of satisfaction elsewhere. Indeed, I have never understood why many managers find it necessary to write, when the same instructions can be passed so much more effectively either in person or over the telephone. I appreciate that the numbers of staff involved may sometimes make a personal approach more difficult, but that is what delegation is all about and, while a confirmation memorandum may indeed still be a necessity, the rule should always be to keep your business dealings as personal as possible, particularly in your relationships with subordinates. The drive for efficiency in a modern office has been responsible for many improvements, but no greater retrograde step has taken place than talking to employees with little bits of paper. As Dean Acheson once said, 'A memorandum is written, not to inform the reader, but to protect the writer.' Those who either fax their instructions on doubtful quality paper or, even worse, send them via a computer screen, are probably past listening to such advice anyway, but if you have not yet reached that stage there is still time to turn back. You were, after all, quite happy to spend time talking to your new employee when you interviewed him for the job, so why stop once you employ him?

COMMUNICATION BY DELEGATION

Ideal communication must be face to face if the two-way traffic of information is to be possible at all, but, however good this is, it is naive to think that this is even remotely practical in the everyday running of a large organisation. Delegation is, of course, part of the answer but unfortunately, information and instruction passed from one to another has a habit of becoming diluted and coloured by the opinions of those who pass it on. Your own communication techniques to your divisional managers may be excellent, but the continuation down the line will only be as good as those divisional managers themselves. Sadly, there are many people who find it either impossible or difficult to communicate and they will often block the flow of information simply because they are incapable of passing it further. Again, to quote George Bernard Shaw, 'their trouble is that they lack the power of conversation, but not the power of speech.'

There are, of course, methods such as circulars, Tannoy systems and the like, but I would class them all as the 'easy' way out and they rarely have any effect other than satisfying the ego of the instigating manager, enabling him to justify himself by saying 'Well, I told everyone what was happening, didn't I?' People must not only be told what they need to know, they must be told so that they understand.

It is a hard fact that there is no easy way of working effectively with staff which does not rely on your ability to communicate down the line. Most people would agree that the best company chairmen are those do just that and who know everyone who is working for them. This is hardly a practical target, but, if you aim for the ideal, you just might achieve the acceptable. Is it really impossible for the chairman of a large company to sit in occasionally, solely as an onlooker, at a works committee meeting, or even at a sports and social meeting, just to get inside the minds of those who are helping him run his company? 'I haven't got the time,' does not sound too valid when morale falls because staff in a company feel that management are no longer interested in their everyday problems.

MORE ABOUT TWO-WAY TRAFFIC

Whatever type of manager you aim to be and whatever business you are controlling, if you work on the practice of directing your staff from a distance (with the emphasis on directing), you will eventually fail because you will have believed that your job is merely a one-way communication line and, like the one-way salesman, you will have little real concept of what the recipient is actually either thinking or wanting. The same errors will creep in if it is one way from your chief executive (or whoever) to yourself as when it is one way between yourself and the staff for whom you are responsible. If you cannot communicate in both directions you will first of all find the evaluation of your job impossible because you are not getting feedback on what is right or wrong, but, more important, you will be losing the value of the knowledge and skills for which you pay good money to your employees. In the case of new recruits in particular, remember how much effort you spent in ensuring that they had the skills that your job requirement demanded and then think how often in practice those skills are ignored.

THE GAP BETWEEN THEORY AND PRACTICE

What is done in practice is rarely the same as what is preached. I worked for a brief period for a company where the theory of the open plan office was implemented, the idea of doors and separate offices being replaced by a large open scheme with no separation between the desks and separate operations. I cannot say that I accept the principle, because that extreme appears to me to create more inefficiency than it solves, but the unbelievable part was that the managing director was separated from the whole confusion by a flight of stairs, and located in an office which was as accessible to staff as Fort Knox. As a result, he knew little of his staff and little of the problems with which they had to deal.

Take that example and extend it to all your activities. Think of your style of communication. Does it represent a door between you and your colleagues which only you can open? If so, then the best move is to unscrew the door at the hinges. At the very least make sure that it is wedged open so that your company personnel are aware that you encourage their participation in what you are doing. Listen as much as you direct, and you will be able to decide whether your directives are valid and indeed acceptable.

GARBAGE IN CIRCULATION

And, while we are looking at the whole question of directives, if you are looking to streamline your communication, whether you are taking over an existing organisation or developing a new one of your own, always check whether the information which is sent from department to department really has any value. Remember there are people who judge the standard of their job by the volume of incoming information and paper which they accumulate on their desks, and those employees will be the last to tell you that what you are sending has no particular use.

Very often requirements change, and what was needed yesterday is no longer needed today, or in fact is needed, not in that department, but in another. It must be the job of the efficient manager to regularly check the flow of paper and figures to make sure that what is produced remains relevant. If you don't take the trouble to check this out, no one else, and certainly not the recipients, will do it for you.

However, in your enthusiasm to cut down on the flow of paper, do not cut off the flow altogether. You will find managers who deliberately do not listen and do not ask for information simply because they are apprehensive of the suggestions and views of their subordinates. They believe that it is easier (which it is) and also more efficient (which it isn't) to send out directives which on paper at least indicate who is the chief and who are the indians. Such people gradually lose the intimate knowledge of their work force that is essential if any company is to work smoothly. To help the flow – leave your door open. (The psychological one as well as the real one). Close it or, even worse, lock it and you will gradually find that no one will even try the handle.

CHECKLIST

- Communication is two way – both upwards and downwards.

- Know your subordinates. Know what they want from their careers and whether they believe they are getting it.

- Ask for opinions and ideas, even if you end up using your own.

- Keep your staff informed on changes and developments in your company. If they are not told what is happening, they will make it up and probably get it wrong.

- Constantly review the information you send out. Is it necessary at all?

- Always be available to those who work for you. They are your bread and butter as much as you are theirs.

8

The art of delegation

' Treat people as if they were what they ought to be, and you help them to become what they are capable of.'

Johann W von Goethe, 1749–1832

On the desk of Harry S Truman, president of the United States in 1945, appeared a brass plate which said 'The Buck Stops Here'. There is no doubt that, considering the job involved, that was a fairly valid claim.

In business, however, the opposite is probably the norm. The way in which delegation traditionally works in a company is that action is passed down the line until eventually it reaches the least important employee who then has no one left to delegate to. Cynical possibly, but in the complex scale of the majority of businesses, delegation is the only way of making sure that you are not bogged down with decisions you have no time to make, and also that your subordinates recognise that they too have a part to play and a responsibility to hold in the decision making of the company.

WHAT IS DELEGATED? RESPONSIBILITY? DECISIONS? BLAME?

It has always seemed to me to be wrong to call for the resignation of the chairman of a large company simply because someone, somewhere down the line, has made an error for which a scapegoat is required. The error *might* have been to delegate to that particular person in the first place, but, having done that, the responsibility is shared and the can for any mistake should surely be carried by the person who made that mistake.

It has long been a definition of delegation that you are not delegating the responsibility, but that you are delegating the decision while still retaining the responsibility yourself. This is a half-way stage which leaves the delegated employee no great authority at all and makes him aware that a bad decision, and the results from it, can then be passed back up the line again. If you delegate, at least make sure that your subordinate is aware that he not only has the authority, but that he will also have to account for the decisions that he makes. You still retain responsibility in that you made the decision to appoint him, but both you and he should be aware that by delegation, you now share the responsibility and are in different degrees answerable for what is done.

There are extremes in the scale of delegation. One is to delegate nothing on the theory that if you make yourself that indispensable, you will never be dispensed with. The second is to delegate everything so that you avoid the risky problem of making a decision for which you might later get blamed. Somewhere in the middle is where you really want to be and is probably the hardest to achieve. But, in your anxiety to get it right, do not just pass across the jobs that you do not wish to do yourself. Delegate properly and you may well regret losing some of your more enjoyable tasks, but your subordinates will think little of you if you merely retain the more interesting jobs and pass over the menial ones. As a last thought, never delegate to someone else the clearing up of a mess of your own making.

SETTING LIMITS FOR DELEGATION

I remember when I was around 25 being told by my sales manager, who was also my office manager, that he was off on a holiday for two weeks and during his absence I was in charge of the London operation. His last words on the Friday evening before his departure were, 'Take all the decisions that I would take and try to get them right. If the decision involves taking a risk which loses the company £1000, I won't complain, but take one which loses £2000 and we might need to talk about it. But, if a problem arises and you take no decision at all, I can assure you that on my return your job will no longer be open.' As delegation it really couldn't be beaten as I had been given pretty accurate perameters within which to work. Fortunately I didn't need to refer to any of the rules I had been given, but in hindsight I know that I was then working for a man who knew how to delegate down the line. If you, as a manager, fail to take any risks in the shape of the decisions of your subordinates, then you may as well not employ competent subordinates at all because you will never be asking them to exercise their talents.

The real art of delegation consists of knowing your staff and their abilities. You must assess how much authority a subordinate actually needs to do his job effectively, and you must then judge how much authority he is capable of coping with, which can often be difficult to determine if he has not handled authority previously. The two may well not be the same, in which case your subordinate has already reached his level of competence, unless, of course, he can be trained to take his actual capabilities further.

There may also be reasons other than the demands on your time, which make it necessary that you delegate, in particular if you as a manager do not have the required specialist skills. You would not, for example, as a sales manager, be expected to have a close working knowledge of computer programming, so you would pass over that particular responsibility to someone qualified to handle it. Again, you transfer the authority but it remains within your responsibility to ensure that the delegated work is correctly carried out.

LEVELS OF DECISION MAKING

In principle, problems should always be dealt with at the lowest level practicable, partly because the decision-maker will then be on a lower salary scale and so the operation is cheaper, and partly because the senior man who delegated the decision then has time to do the real job for which he is being paid. If all problems and decisions are handled at the top, or near the top, as they were in one company for which I worked, the organisation tends to come to a standstill, stifled because ideas are not encouraged, initiative is not expected and the time of expensive executives is taken up with matters which could easily have been dealt with by a clerk or secretary. If you adopt the same policy, do not be surprised if you have little time to do the important work for which you are being paid.

Do not forget also that in your policy on delegation, you must look closely at the administrative clutter which inevitably lands on any good manager's desk. You need to avoid the standard manager's complaint that 'I do not have the time'. Ask yourself if you really do not have the time or do you say that out of habit and then proceed to get on with a job which could easily have been done by someone else. Always remember that if you are disorganised, then most of the people around you, because they rely on you, will be disorganised also, so making your initial problem worse than it was before.

THE ROLE OF A SECRETARY

If you merely regard your secretary as a typist, or as someone who is unable to make decisions and accept responsibility, then you have either employed the wrong person or, worse still, you are not making use of the talents which are at your elbow.

A good secretary, well informed about the business that you are in, and given a degree of authority to make decisions, can be of inestimable value to any new manager who is coming to terms with the new responsibilities that he has inherited. Think of the hard work that you or your predecessor put in to recruit a secretary who had all the talents that your company was looking for and then ask why in so many companies those talents are just not used. A fear of relinquishing authority is often the real reason why a manager insists that decisions, which could easily be taken by the person on the spot, are sometimes left until the manager returns.

A secretary should be able (and encouraged) to make basic decisions which would otherwise have been placed on your desk. A good working relationship should ensure that the decisions made would be the same as you would have made yourself. Even if your secretary has not yet secured your total confidence, it must surely be worth taking the occasional risk to ensure that your in-tray is not filled with papers which are of medium importance to your company. The more of this kind of work which can be answered or even transferred to the department who should have dealt with it in the first place, the more time you will have for the management of sales which should be the main priority of your job.

OBJECTIONS FROM ANTI-DELEGATORS

The objections to delegating at all are many and are used regularly by managers who are uncertain of their own ability either to delegate or to control those to whom they do delegate.

'The customers always want to see a senior manager'

This is nonsense as customers generally want to see someone who can give them the time that they believe they deserve. It may be necessary to allocate the company representative a better title so that the customer ego is not damaged, but in the end the customer will still be happier if the person with whom he is dealing has the authority (delegated) to handle the sale or the problem. The hotel industry has long held this view, which is why almost everyone in the hotel business is an assistant manager.

'I can do the job more quickly by myself'

Possibly true, in which case it is about time you trained someone else to your level of competence. Remember that no one is indispensable, and skills are easily acquired by someone who has the ability and the enthusiasm.

'If he makes a mess of it, I will be the one who needs to explain the failure to the directors'

You probably will, but do it the other way and you might also need to explain why you did not get time to do the job at all. You might also need to explain why you appointed the wrong person to do the job in the first place. Had you taken more care in your choice neither problem would have arisen.

'If I pass major decisions over, I will lose control of the day-to-day running of what I am meant to be doing'

Again we are back to communication to ensure that you know what is being done and retain influence over how it is done. The whole process of delegation is designed to lift the everyday running of a division or department from a manager, while still leaving him with the overall responsibility of making sure that the job is efficiently carried out.

'Others haven't got the necessary skills'

Then train them or replace them. The skill is probably there already, the average company usually failing to recognise and use the talent which is available. 'Work in any company is achieved by those employees who have not yet reached their level of incompetence' (Dr Laurence J Peter).

Lastly, when you do delegate, remember that you have made a decision. Continually going back to check the work is a lack of confidence, not just in the subordinate, but also in yourself and the decision that you have made. Once you have passed the buck, leave it there. If you don't, you need not be surprised when you eventually get it passed back.

CHECKLIST

- When you delegate, you pass a good part of the responsibility also.
- Failure to delegate is as irresponsible as delegating everything.
- Give yourself time by properly using the talents of others.
- Back your confidence in others by leaving them to do the jobs they have been given.

9

Hold meetings and sales conferences for the right reasons

' To get something done, a committee should consist of no more than three men, two of them absent.'

Dr Laurence J Peter

TYPES OF MEETINGS AND THOSE WHO ATTEND THEM

You will often hear the opinion expressed by those who should know better, 'Meetings are all a waste of time', and while this is regrettably based on experience of meetings which have been a waste of time, it must also be true that properly run meetings are vital to the running of a company or organisation. Somewhere in the middle the good manager needs to find a compromise between these two extremes. It is not easy.

You will encounter two types of participants: first, those who attend meetings simply because they like them, and anyway it makes them seem more important than they really are; and, secondly, those who dislike meetings, avoid them whenever they can, and in doing so fail to pass on to others their own skills and knowledge. The latter are unfortunately often the ones who contribute when they do attend and are essential if any meeting is to have any value at all.

We are really talking about two kinds of meetings in which you will be involved. First, there are the management meetings where personnel involved in different areas of the company are brought together to decide company policy. In meetings like this, you may either call them or be called to them, and the amount of influence you may have will inevitably be controlled by which of those two options it is. Either way, the object of such meetings is to take decisions and implement them, and rarely are the participants brought together merely to inform them of changes in company policy or possibly products.

The second type of meeting falls into the category of sales meeting or sales conference, the essential difference between the two being that of size. In this second type of meeting, decisions are not likely to be taken, and they are principally designed to inform and to bring together those who need to be informed. The object of any meeting may be to put out information, externally or internally, such as to a union work force meeting or to a press conference, or indeed it might be a marketing orientated meeting such as a sales seminar or convention specifically involved in a product launch or a review of past performance. It is important to look at the two basic types of meeting and recognise the different ways in which each should be handled.

MANAGEMENT MEETINGS

For management meetings at which decisions will be made, you will either be responsible for calling the meeting or merely (I use the word advisedly) be responsible for attending. Either way there will have been an agenda (prepared by you or someone else) and in any meeting a considerable amount of time can always be saved if pressure is put on the participants to look at the agenda beforehand and decide how, if at all, they can contribute to what is going to be discussed. It is largely because this is not done that meetings often become the personal platform of the person who called them and the value of any contributions from others is often lost. If meetings in your company invariably appear a waste of time, it could well be because the format could be forecast long before the meeting takes place and rarely are decisions taken which someone in authority has not already decided.

Hold meetings and sales conferences for the right reasons

Meetings should always be designed for discussion and for an intelligent exchange of views between those in a company with different skills and, of course, different viewpoints. As Robert Quiller says, 'Discussion is an exchange of knowledge, argument an exchange of ignorance.' If those attending either have no view about something, or alternatively have a view and are wary of expressing it, then you have immediately lost the value of the experience they have accumulated or have brought with them from another company. It does happen and is probably the main reason why the opinion that 'meetings are a waste of time' is so often heard.

The traditional cynical description of a meeting is of a group of people who individually are incapable of doing anything, but together are capable of deciding that nothing can be done. This really says it all and if meetings really are like that, then there is every reason for not holding them in the future. However, if you can avoid the pitfalls which lead to non-decision making, you will probably be half-way to ensuring that meetings are welcomed as a means of solving problems rather than extending them.

OBJECTIONS TO MEETINGS

It might, therefore, be helpful to look at the reasons that people give for not holding meetings so that those particular stumbling blocks can be recognised and eliminated.

- Meetings waste the time of those who attend them and those who have to act on decisions made at them. Other methods of making decisions would be more effective.

- Meetings are designed to provide a platform for those who want to establish their authority. This, of course, means the chairman who called the meeting in the first place.

- Meetings are an official channel for passing the buck.

- Meetings are the launch pad for sub-committees which are set up to deal with problems that should have been dealt with by the managers paid to deal with them.

If you can succeed in eliminating these particular objections, you will then have established a justification for the meeting in the first place. What is the main reason why people say that a meeting is a waste of time?

To avoid the participants regarding a meeting as having been a waste of time, it is necessary for the convenor to have a clear idea of its purpose, to ask himself – 'Why have a meeting in the first place?' I once worked for a company who always had a management meeting on Monday mornings. Not because there was anything specific to discuss (except the minutes of the previous meeting), but because it was Monday morning. It would be difficult to imagine a more guaranteed way of ensuring that the participants emerged saying, 'Well, that was all a waste of time', than sending them into a meeting where there was no particular object to achieve by being there.

The only reason for a meeting, apart from those where company law determines, as for a board meeting, that you must hold one, must be to discuss something which cannot be dealt with any other way. And yet, in company after company, meetings are held on a regular basis where, for instance, the parts manager will reel off his turnover to everyone else, the sales manager will give his figures to the parts manager (and everyone else), and a general discussion will take place on matters which could (and should) have been left to the departmental heads responsible for them. Minutes are then taken and, one week later, the whole tedious process is repeated.

There are, of course, situations where a mutual use of each other's expertise is demanded before a decision can be reached. If that decision can be taken by one person with his own knowledge and skills, then there is really no need for a meeting at all and a note to tell interested parties what he has done, if even that is necessary, will serve the same purpose. If, after that, someone who is affected by that decision feels that further discussion would be helpful, then fine, for you have the basis for a meeting to be called to discuss it and you are then moving into the area where you use meetings effectively rather than let them use you.

IN FAVOUR OF MEETINGS

There are certain less obvious advantages that a meeting will offer. In particular, the value of communication, both upwards and downwards, cannot be minimised, especially when that communication is between people who do not normally meet. However, where that communication does not affect the decision which is made, and where the views of participants are not heeded, the holding of a meeting is a guaranteed way of ensuring that people who attend it leave with the view that it was all a waste of time.

There is probably an alternative way of achieving the communication advantage (which is an essential ingredient in the team spirit of a company) than holding a meeting, since that, on its own, is no reason for holding a meeting in the first place. The principal purpose for a meeting must be contained in the agenda, to explain why everyone is being called together. If no reason is given, other than to discuss the meeting which was held last week, and to update the figures which were given on that occasion, then do not be too surprised if your people attend with the same lack of purpose that you had yourself in calling it. To quote GK Chesterton, 'It isn't that they can't see the solution. It is that they can't see the problem.'

THE AGENDA

The agenda is, of course, a relatively formal schedule and has, for the most part, a format which experience has proved to be well tried and effective. It will usually list reasons why some people have not turned up (Apologies for Absence). It will confirm what was said last time (The Minutes) and will try to put to bed certain matters which were left overhanging from the last meeting (Matters Arising). It will then outline what is to be discussed that day so that anyone with a relevant opinion can come prepared to express it and, having done all of that, it will prompt discussion on whether, or if, the next meeting should take place. The agenda must, obviously, be clear, circulated well before the meeting and personnel who are expected to make a particular contribution must be individually advised as to what is expected of them. If you can, time the agenda so that participants know how much of their day it is likely to take, so that they can plan their other duties. A good chairman should also monitor the flow of a meeting to ensure that there is proper discussion time allocated to all agenda items.

The one area where time-wasting is not only guaranteed, but is even encouraged is the customary final phrase, 'Any Other Business', a phrase which, in my opinion, should be deleted from the programme of all meetings, both social and business.

If a matter being raised is really so unimportant that it could not be raised beforehand and inserted in the agenda, then it should not be included at all, and the 'Any Other Business' time merely gives an opportunity to those who have not contributed to any other part of the meeting to carry out a personal bit of tub thumping. In addition they will raise matters which come as a surprise to all the others who arrive unprepared to discuss them.

I know it is a difficult deletion to make, as 'Any Other Business' appears on every agenda sheet from John O'Groats to Lands End, but surely there must be some way of removing this one particular time-waster from the programme. After all, if there is really a matter which becomes topical, and important, at a late stage prior to the meeting, and is considered by the chairman to be worthy of discussion, an amended agenda can be issued to include it, so that the participants at the meeting have the ability to do their own research on the subject before the meeting actually begins.

Again, if you do not feel that this aspect is important and do not intend to research a subject, or indeed offer a contribution to the topics being raised, then you are probably going to be one of those who will *always* find meetings a waste of time.

SALES MEETINGS

Having dealt with the management meetings which will be part of your regular administrative week, and having hopefully put them into a format which means that they are productive, we now must consider the other kind of meetings which are part of your sales function and which, for reasons other than merely discussion, will be essential on a regular basis. Such meetings are designed for a different purpose entirely and will usually be planned to bring together people, who, because of their geographical locations, would not often meet. There will no doubt be a particular prime purpose for such meetings and they will also be expensive to organise. Consequently they must be more skilfully planned and set up to achieve the result you are aiming for. A key element of the response you are looking for will be enthusiasm.

The starting point is the same. There must be a reason for calling it, not simply because you always have a sales meeting at this time of year. People must come to the meeting knowing why it is being held so that they are prepared, if necessary, with information which will help them make their own contribution. The reason might be a little more contrived than before, particularly as you need the meeting anyway to develop your communication with salesmen in the field, but a reason must certainly be the starting point. A sales conference will often develop a 'theme' to give more meat to the reason for holding it, but the object is the same, to inform delegates why they are there.

You have, of course, cheaper options if all you wish you do is to provide the salesmen with information; in planning your sales meeting you must work hard to ensure that the expensive option of a sales meeting succeeds in providing the advantages that the cheaper options do not.

All delegates must be contributors

Any meeting must involve those attending, not just as listeners but also as participants. While such meetings are not looking for decisions from the floor, they are certainly looking for contributions which will, if they do nothing else, help weld your people together into a team who are aware that their suggestions and opinions are taken seriously. I recognise the truth of the proverb, 'They say most who have least to say', but sometimes, at the other extreme, you will need to work at bringing into the open those who are happier just to sit and listen.

The methods developed from 'brainstorming' in the United States are techniques which can well be encouraged, ensuring that as many people as possible contribute to an 'ideas' session, out of which the useful material can be extracted and later discussed. Sometimes these brainstorming sessions can be run on their own, but, within a regular sales meeting, they can often encourage contributions from those who might otherwise be reluctant to offer their opinions. Alternatively, advise delegates that they will each be asked to contribute one suggestion, however simple, aimed at improving business. A brainstorming meeting will usually deal with only one topic and it is essential that all ideas, whether laughable or improbable, are thrown into the ring without any immediate criticism from others. Criticism merely stifles the flow of ideas which is the prime purpose of the session. One warning must be made. Well handled, a brainstorming meeting can produce ideas which might develop into useful projects. Badly handled, a brainstorming meeting is more likely to be labelled a time-waster than any other.

Use presentation aids

If you are launching a new product or service, you will have, at a meeting of this type, full opportunity to use audio/visual aids giving advantages that the memorandum from head office can never hope to. It is essential that you design your meeting to use all these facilities, such as flip boards and projected presentations which are not available to you in your normal environment.

Encourage salesmen to exchange intelligence

Make sure that communication between salesmen, not easily available in the field, is used to exchange information which might be useful to others. Very often at such sales meetings, the communication is all from the manager or the lectern, and proper use is not made of the talents of the more successful salesmen to guide those who may have less experience. In addition to the actual training value that is gained, there will also be considerable advantage in involving in the management process personnel who might not normally consider themselves part of it.

Choose a non-office venue

You will, of course, have to select your venue to suit the people who are going to attend, but, in order to save cost, do not, unless it is absolutely essential, hold your meeting on your company's premises. For many reasons, if only to avoid the problem that the managers who are attending will regard their regular responsibilities as something they can 'slip out to' whenever they have time, it is essential that your meeting is held away from the distractions presented by the normal office environment. If you calculate the overall cost of bringing people from all over an area into one place, the cost is increased only marginally by hiring a room to accommodate them when they get there. Generally anyway, the provision of a meeting room in a hotel will probably be free if you intend to use the facilities of the hotel for lunch.

Seating arrangements

When you have decided on your venue, it will be an important part of your responsibility to decide how you want the seating, as this will often determine the kind of co-operation you get from the floor. Don't leave decisions like that to your own staff or even to the hotel organisers, as the results may well determine whether your conference or meeting is a success or a failure. Arrange the seating classroom style and that is just the sort of reaction you will get from the participants. Arrange the same seating so that everyone feels that they are encouraged to take part and they will do so a great deal more freely. If you are planning a slide presentation or a video display, two long lines of salesmen down the sides of a table will ensure that all each salesman can see is the back of the salesman in front, and all you will see during the later discussion, is the salesman nearest to you. You can be assured that those who prefer to hide will swiftly do so if there is someone or something behind which they can lose themselves. For any meeting to be a success, you want contributions from as many of those attending as possible.

If the aim of your meeting is to talk to your audience, then the seating arrangement makes little difference, but if you wish the audience to talk to you, then you must encourage flow of speech.

TO SUM UP . . .

There is no way that the many possibilities of conducting a meeting can be covered in one chapter and the actual format will, anyway, be so subjective and so different depending on the reasons on why the meeting was called, that a set of rules which is good for all occasions is not going to be found. However as in selling, the best guidelines of all come back to the use of empathy and the skill in setting up the kind of meeting at which the participants feel comfortable and are consequently prepared to contribute in the way you want them to. Fail to provide all the physical assistance you can, in the way of room layout, presentation of written information, good prior information on why the meeting is being held and how long it is likely to last, and you will have contributed to the participants feeling that they would have been better off staying at home.

CHECKLIST

- 'Waste of time meetings' are usually badly planned meetings.
- Management meetings must have a reason for being called and an agenda to say what that reason is.
- Those attending meetings are there not just to listen, but also to contribute.
- Forget 'Any other business' – the guaranteed time-waster.
- Sales meetings must be designed to generate enthusiasm. That is why they are held. If all you achieve is the passing on of information, a memo would have done it better.

10

Developing the skills of your personnel

' Sixty years ago, I knew everything; now I know nothing. Education is a progressive discovery of our own ignorance.'

Will Durant

NEW STAFF NEED SETTLING IN

It is a known fact that if there is dissatisfaction with the job, it often starts very early on in the careers of newly joined personnel. No new employee really lacks enthusiasm on his first day since most join with the right motives, but that enthusiasm is often killed simply because a certain standard of education and reception is expected but rarely achieved. The induction system, even on the first day, is frequently badly handled because the manager who employed the new recruit fails to make arrangements for a training plan to ensure that those first few days are properly organised.

An employer must recognise that a new employee is *just* that. New to the firm, new to its methods of working, new to the geography and facilities of the premises, and new to the personnel with whom he will be working. To go through all the extended business of interview and selection, and then to allow only a few hours, or at worst a few minutes, to get settled in the job, is not merely unreasonable, but it is also expensive in that it generates a dissatisfied recruit who may become very swiftly disenchanted with the move that he has made. Yet the mistake is made and made regularly, and it is important that the induction of an employee into a new position is regarded as seriously as the training which should follow it.

TRAINING MATTERS

Training has a particular importance in selling that it has in few other departments of your company. Your front-line sales personnel are inevitably isolated from the head office control centre and they will generally spend far more time with their customers than they will with their own colleagues. As a consequence, the head office influence will be minimal compared with the opinions of those outside the company and in particular with the opinions of those customers who may well criticise your company for actions which it interprets as failings. It is essential, for that reason, that training, in-house or otherwise, is planned into the schedule of every one of your salesmen so that they are regularly re-vitalised with the principles and policies of your own company, and the loyalty that is expected from the salesmen towards those policies. This is not just setting out the responsibilities of the selling job that they are doing, but must inevitably also involve the image and reputation that the company is aiming to promote. It is mainly because the Japanese are so disciplined in such matters that they succeed in installing intense loyalty in their staff.

In addition, there are very few of your sales force, and that includes the experienced high fliers, who cannot learn from regularly programmed courses in selling techniques and product knowledge and, while such courses are recognised practice for most new employees, they are often considered unnecessary for more experienced staff. Remember that such courses are probably most needed by those who claim that they have nothing to learn from them.

THE TRAINING FUNCTION

Training in a big company is, of course, often handled by a completely separate division and the planning of it may very well be carried out by that division, not by your own. However, while in such a company you probably would not have the time to handle much of the actual training yourself, it is important that the sales aspects of that programme are set by you, and that the standard you expect to come out of that programme is clearly defined and monitored.

The passing of information on the product or service can certainly be left to others, but in the end you will need to be regarded as the expert on the selling techniques which are relevant to your particular sales operation and it must be your own responsibility to ensure that the standards you need are those that are actually set. It is often too easy to leave that standard to others who might have a very different idea from you on what is required. In addition, sales training will usually take place as much in the field as in the classroom and even if you are not directly responsible for the second, you will certainly be responsible for the first.

You must ensure that all employees have a fixed training programme and that they know in advance what it is. The casual 'pick it up as you go along' approach, known as the 'Sit by Nellie' method, is not only ineffective but also indicates to the trainee just how little regard you have for the position that he has been given. Training should also be ongoing, meaning that it is not simply a policy which applies to new personnel but is in place throughout the career of any employee to ensure that his level of ability is constantly being upgraded. In the last century, General Robert E Lee is quoted as saying that 'the education of a man is never completed until he dies', and in business too, training must be continuous. A one-off course produces, like a Chinese meal, a great sense of satisfaction both during and immediately afterwards, but be assured that the satisfaction does not last unless your personnel really feel that they are part of a system that is constantly aimed at upgrading their capabilities.

In addition to the special attention that you will give to new employees, a constant watch must also be kept on the qualities of all the personnel who are working for you and on whom you will rely to carry out your plans. Are your people capable of handling their responsibilities or will you have to look outside your organisation for those you will need in the future? If you are to retrain you will need to be planning well ahead of the jobs that your personnel are being retrained for. If, also, you become too reliant on one or two key people, you run the risk that you will be thrown into chaos if those key people should up and leave you for one of your competitors.

Have you given thought to training and developing younger personnel to take over when you either retire or lose the enthusiasm and drive you had when you started? Are your personnel trained to develop new ideas rather than merely keep the old systems rolling? Is the office equipment that is available modern and are you making use of new technology? It is little use to have staff trained in modern methods, but without the machinery necessary to implement them. This is all part of training and you will need to match those facilities to the pressures that higher sales will bring.

When looking for new staff, you will need to establish the qualities that your selling policy will demand and then, once you know that, you must decide how technically qualified your candidates need to be. Having done that, you can decide whether your training facilities are capable of raising your own personnel to that level or indeed whether you have the time to do so. The alternative is to pay the price for buying someone who already has the skills that you require and who will be expected to be well paid for bringing those skills to you.

PLANNING TRAINING COURSES

As a sales manager, whether your company has its own training department or not, you will be closely involved in the planning and content of any courses which are set up. This is the one area where, apart from your work with the sales force in the field, you have the ability to pass on your knowledge and experience, and also to use the experience of others in your organisation who are capable of training both new and existing personnel. There are, of course, outside consultants who will take your staff from you and train them in their own colleges, but it is in your own company that you need to make your plans. If you rely on others to do your training for you, the one great advantage which will be missing is the continual emphasis on your own company name and reputation and the image that you wish to create for that company with your employees. Carry out your training in-house and you will be able to develop that image in a way that can only be of benefit to your company.

The type of training that you plan can only be determined by what you are selling, but, if you are either looking to overhaul existing facilities, or need to set up an organisation from scratch, then a few guidelines will be of help.

Tell – show – do

In all training, there is a set pattern to aim for and, while different situations will have different demands, the 'tell', 'show' and 'do' approach is, without question, the one which will implant in the minds of the trainees the skills you are trying to teach. 'Tell', on its own, is a weak way of instructing anyone. It can be done verbally, by writing or even by correspondence course, but the absorption rate is low if it is not followed by 'Show', with some demonstration by the trainer of what is required. This may be actual or by video, but unless the trainee forms a visual picture of the instructions that have been given, there will be far less likelihood that, at the end of it all, he will retain what he has been told. And lastly, he must then carry out the operation himself, 'Do' – to prove to himself, or the trainer, that he has understood and absorbed the skill, and has the ability to carry it out.

The training location

If the geography of your premises is not suitable for training the people you anticipate, then move your training location elsewhere. This need be neither permanent nor even involve anything other than hiring an appropriate room for the day, but it is simply bad management to occupy the time of your instructors or senior staff by using an environment which is not only unsuitable, but also does little to convey to the personnel attending, the importance you attach to the training itself. In addition, it is often sensible to arrange that location away from your usual place of work as that will minimise the interruptions that will always occur when alternative distractions are too close to hand.

Brief the trainers

You will, of course, be drawing in other personnel who will be presenting their own skills to the trainees. Make sure, well in advance, what programme you are expecting those personnel to cover and how long a period you expect them to be responsible for. Find out what facilities they need, whether it be slide projectors, flip boards or whatever, and ensure that everyone is aware whose responsibility it is to provide them. Make sure that senior personnel know that your arrangements, once made, have total priority over all else.

Prepare accompanying course notes

Arrange, whatever topic is being covered, that relevant course notes are prepared and delivered to the trainees in a professional looking folder or ring binder which can be retained for subsequent reference. Photocopied notes on single sheets of paper are rarely looked at after the course is over and any time spent on making their presentation more attractive will enhance the reputation of your company and increase the chance of the information being read again another day. It is preferable if these notes are not given to the trainees until after the lecture to which they refer and that all trainees should be encouraged to make their own notes throughout simply to concentrate their minds on remembering what is being said.

Outside speakers provide variation

Outside speakers, with no everyday connection with your company, are often useful in providing a different approach to what you are aiming to put across and can often, particularly if they come from your own suppliers, be acquired at little or no cost. It is always one of the problems of any training course that the subject matter and presentation tend to be the prerogative of a limited number of your own personnel, and an ability to expand and broaden the perspective of your subject matter can prove very rewarding.

TRAINING ... ENOUGH'S ENOUGH

Lastly, in all training and assessment, you, as a manager, now have a duty, not just to provide training, but also to evaluate those who are getting it and to decide whether there is a point where you must cut your losses and train no more. There are people who are in the wrong job, either because you inherited them with that problem or because you made a mistake in appointing them, and there will be occasions where you will need to dismiss personnel, not because of a lack or motivation or enthusiasm, but simply because they cannot carry out the job they were given. No one can be blamed and in those cases, a decision to dismiss and start again is probably the only one available to you. More training is no answer, although it is often used to delay a decision which is probably long overdue anyway. The error, if an error was made, was in appointing the person in the first place and whether this was your original decision or not is largely irrelevant. It will certainly be your problem to solve and many bad personnel appointments are prolonged by the optimistic expectation that if you send someone on enough courses, he will eventually secure the right knowledge and skill to do the job. Trying to turn a non-salesman into a salesman will certainly be a time-waster and will probably be unsuccessful also. 'Who knows, he might improve', may be all right for your first assessment of an employee, but it is certainly wrong for the second assessment and thereafter.

CHECKLIST

- With any new employee, training must start on day one and be planned for the rest of his career.
- As sales manager, the responsibility for the content of sales training is yours. This is one thing you cannot delegate.
- Constantly monitor the progress and demands of your sales team, and ensure that their talents are developed by adequate training.
- Recognise when your salesmen have reached their level of competence. You cannot train people into jobs for which they are not suited.

Motivating the sales force

'The deepest principle of human nature is the craving to be appreciated.'

William James

ENCOURAGEMENT WORKS WONDERS

There will be few who do not accept that motivation in all forms of employment is vital. In the sales operation, however, you have more problems in developing and motivating your personnel than in any other. Salesmen in the field do not have the advantages of regular contact with others in their company, and is it easy for them to feel that they are out on a limb with little reaction to the success of the work that they are doing. They are well aware that they will get reaction to failure, but you will find that it is a regular complaint from the field that recognition of achievement is a great deal rarer than it should be.

You may well be lucky and employ a salesman who is happy to work without encouragement, who regards his salary and commission as the only incentives he needs, and who also has no ambition to advance in his job beyond the position that he has. However, it is far more likely that a failure on your part to recognise the other demands of your salesman will result in his looking elsewhere for an alternative appointment, giving as his explanation one of the following reasons.

- 'I just do not get the right back-up from my present company.'
- 'Managers are always appointed from outside the company and there is no real chance of advancement.'

- 'I never seem to be told where my present job is leading me.'
- 'There is no regular training programme and I am always left to find out new developments for myself. No one seems interested in building on the skills that I can offer.'
- 'The management never seem really involved and are unable to give praise when it is due.'
- 'Figures are never discussed with the employees involved, except in a critical way and often unreasonable targets are set without reference to those who are being asked to achieve them.'

If some of the above comments seem familiar, and may even have been made by you in the past, you can be certain that anything that you can do to ensure that they are not said by your own salesmen will be time well spent. Motivation is necessary to get the best of the personnel under your control, and unless you look at all the ways that staff are motivated and at all the ways that their morale is depressed, you can find that your sales figures are low, not because you are employing the wrong salesmen, but because you have the right salesmen and are not using their talents correctly. Part of your policy towards your staff must always be to make sure that the qualities of your existing staff are properly evaluated for it is certainly true that no one's true worth is recognised until that person resigns. It is worth while remembering that if you can induce others to work for you by offering attractive incentives to do so, then your own existing employees are at risk if you fail to make sure that their reward packages reflect their own talents and experience.

It is a sad thought that salesmen are easily tempted to work at a lower level than they are capable of simply because there is little supervision, and because the enthusiasm with which they started their job is not encouraged and sustained throughout their career. Motivation, of whatever kind, should not be planned to drive your sales force to achievements beyond their capability, but it should certainly be designed to ensure that the morale of the sales team is continually strengthened and maintained, and that they are aware that management shares the problems they experience in the field.

ASPECTS OF MOTIVATION

It need not always cost money, although money will come into the scheme somewhere, but motivation includes, for instance, writing a letter (not a duplicated memo) to a successful salesman congratulating him on a particular order or a particular achievement. If a special comment is called for, then greater impact can be achieved if the letter comes from a director who would not normally write, even by memo, to that employee. If in the process you are recognising also that your employee has a higher capability than you previously thought, then acknowledge that by passing down to him more authority to handle matters that you might previously have restricted to yourself.

Motivate, if you can, with praise. In the words of George Bernard Shaw, 'The worst sin against our fellow man is not to hate him but to be indifferent to him.' React in this way to the successes of your salesmen and do not be surprised if you destroy the motivation they had in working for you.

The main principle of any scheme is that you must know what motivates a salesman and each is different. The carrot in front of a donkey is fine because the donkey is not clever enough to decide it doesn't like carrots, but offer the same kind of fixed incentive to every salesman on your list and don't be surprised if four out of every ten decide that, for them at least, that particular offering has no attraction at all.

There will be many who flounder when it comes to offering motivation, and have little idea what encourages and what has no effect at all. Unfortunately, the whole question of motivation is so subjective that it is difficult to find any one carrot which appeals to everyone and it is consequently equally difficult to establish a policy which is a winner. As Peter Drucker says, 'We know nothing about motivation. All we can do is write books about it.' Not, I hope, strictly true, but if your method of motivation is wrong, and many are, your sales force will not merely stand still but, even worse, will become demotivated and lose the drive which they need for the future. It is probably true to say that there are not many really lazy employees in the world, although they may well seem so. What you *will* find are disinterested employees, demotivated employees and others who have become apparently lazy simply because they have not been given the incentive to give proper enthusiasm to their jobs.

You must also know what demotivates your staff as if you get that part of it wrong, you will have to offer even more to your personnel to regenerate enthusiasm and morale to an acceptable level. There are many reasons why staff become demotivated but probably most important of all is the poor presentation either of targets, expectations or working conditions which are immediately interpreted by the employee as unreasonable or unacceptable. You will find this dealt with separately in Chapter 5, but it will generally be listed as the prime complaint by those salesmen who find fault with the jobs that they are doing. A close second complaint will almost certainly be a lack of communication and leadership from their direct management, coupled with a lack of praise and encouragement when a particularly successful operation has been completed.

You may, of course, need to direct your salesmen's efforts to particular areas where your company has a short-term need, possibly to compensate for over-production or, for instance, to target a particularly profitable market where the company has not been before. In these cases, it will not be general enthusiasm that you are aiming to generate, but it will be the direction of energies so that they match up with the short or long-term policies of the company.

MOTIVATION IN SALES TRAINING

Under motivation it is important also not to forget the important factor of sales training, which, while it is dealt with elsewhere in this book, must be considered a vital element in persuading a sales employee, and particularly a sales employee out in the field, that the company has an interest in what he is doing (other than the sales figures which his territory is producing). It is very easy for a salesman to feel that he is working in a completely isolated environment and being brought in from that environment to learn new skills, or to revise old ones, can very often operate as a highly effective means of motivation.

ALTERNATIVES FOR MOTIVATING SALESMEN

The options which are available to the sales manager are as follows.

Financial incentives

You can, of course, rely on salary or commission and base your motivation solely on financial incentives. You will, anyway, need a remuneration of some sort and many will tell you that commission is all the incentive which is required. Certainly the American influence has been important in setting up commission-only arrangements, where if you do not sell you do not earn. While arrangements such as this certainly have a place (and they have the advantage that they are easy to implement), financial reward alone is an inadequate reason for working at 110 per cent and moreover creates a sales force whose loyalty is based solely on cash, an easy basis for your competitors to upstage.

In principle, the rule of motivation is that reward must be linked to achievement, but also that employees who are expecting reward in this way must be convinced that a fair system is being used to evaluate individual performance. It is probably this aspect above all which makes most bonus methods both suspect and ineffective since, while numerical achievement, say actual turnover, is easy to classify, the varying effort to acquire it is not.

New challenges can help

A challenge in the job you are doing, linked to a financial reward, will often be quoted as a reason for the success of a highly motivated salesman and, there is truth that an over-familiarity, either with a product you have been selling for years or alternatively with a method of selling which has never changed, can affect the enthusiasm of a salesman to sell as effectively as you would like.

The moral is that fresh challenges generate new enthusiasm.

Your drive and enthusiasm can be infectious

You must also make sure that your own drive and personality get through to the sales force and that your salesmen work well simply because you have created an environment which encourages it.

To a great extent, motivation of any employee depends on his respect for you and his own personal drive to do the job so that it meets with your approval. This is probably the most difficult situation to achieve, but it is certainly the most durable when it is gauged against keeping personnel and encouraging others to join you or your company.

Your preferred option will fall somewhere within these three, but in practice it will only be a mixture of them which will have any result at all and it will be up to you to decide how that mixture is put together. It will, unfortunately, be a different element in that mixture which will be the most important for each of your salesmen, and the subjective nature of that will make it essential that you know how each one reacts to what you are offering.

HOW TO CHOOSE THE CARROTS

So, what is going to be important to your staff and what are they likely to regard as important factors in your treatment of them?

It is not difficult to list factors which are likely to encourage your employees to work harder (motivation) and others which lead them to lose that enthusiasm (demotivation). There are many consultants whose businesses have been built by offering such advice and, while I accept that a rigid scale to work on would be extremely helpful to management, in practice the good sales manager must look for a tailored system and know what each member of his sales force needs to keep him on track. This knowledge may well be with a field sales manager or an area manager, but the knowledge must be there to ensure that each salesman in the field receives the carrot which is right for him. The other alternative, and the easy one, is to throw all the carrots on the floor, the sales commission, the incentive holiday, the personal praise and hope that out of the confusion each salesman will pick up the motivation which is right for him. This can only be called management by luck.

You will not, of course, if you do it correctly, need to alter the kind of remuneration you give to each member of staff and it would be extremely impractical to do so, but you will certainly need to alter the emphasis you place on the various alternatives you are offering.

However, I would question whether there will be many in the field who would place acknowledgement of success very far down the list. I also believe that many managers would be surprised at the low importance that financial reward has in the motivation scale, not because people do not welcome it, but because, without the other carrots, it simply does not motivate on its own.

THE SALES INCENTIVE SCHEME

If you are to consider sales incentive schemes, you will have little difficulty in being offered an impossible variety from which to make your selection. Many businesses have set themselves to operate incentive schemes. They offer travel programmes to almost any part of the world, plans which offer catalogue prizes under points schemes and many individual day or weekend holidays often linked with some kind of national or international event. The list is endless, but the essential ingredient must be that the prize is something which the winner would not normally either consider or be able to afford and, if possible, it should also be original and not merely a repeat of what has already been offered by your competitors in the same line of business. The scheme can be designed simply to increase sales or, as indicated above, to direct sales into one particular area of the market. It may be to encourage new customers or even to rescue old customers, whose loyalty for one reason or another has gone elsewhere.

To be most effective, an incentive scheme should be specific to a particular side of your business or to a particular product which needs promoting over the others and indeed any scheme which is specific in this way will usually be more successful than one which merely attempts to increase turnover over the broad range of your product offerings.

The other essential is to use the incentive scheme over a short period, probably no longer than six to eight weeks. Over a shorter period than this, there has really been little enough time to get the plan launched, while over a longer period, you will have difficulty in sustaining the enthusiasm and after the initial impact has passed you will find that your sales force will quickly relax back to their normal methods. In addition, the longer schemes have the disadvantage that in a competitive situation, where you are playing one salesman off against another, you may well have an obvious winner very early on, and so destroy the enthusiasm and competitive spirit that you are trying to encourage. To offset the last problem, it is often worthwhile to have as many prizes as possible so that even those who, because of the quality of their territory or their sales skill, are unlikely to secure the major prize, can still become involved in a lesser prize and have the satisfaction of securing some additional reward for their selling efforts.

CHECKLIST

- Motivation is encouragement, by whatever means.
- Motivation is subjective. Each salesman will see it differently and will have different motivational triggers.
- A lack of motivation can often be the result of a lack of communication.
- Your salary structure must be properly designed and, if necessary, redesigned. If it doesn't motivate, it is wrong.
- Incentive schemes are often short term, but can be effective.

12

Efficient use of advertising and exhibitions

'Advertising may be described as the science of arresting the human intelligence long enough to get money from it.'

Stephen Leacock

ADVERTISING

Advertising may or may not come under your direct control, but you will certainly need to have a strong influence on the type of promotion which is being used. In many companies publicity and media advertising is handled with little reference to both marketing and sales functions, and as a result costly presentations are often prepared with little real knowledge of the people who are due to be influenced by them. Your advertising department or agency, if you have one, will be skilled in preparing visually attractive material, but may often lack the expertise to emphasise the features which your customers actually want to hear about.

Unless your career background has already included advertising, you are likely to be only on the fringe of a professional practice which, for the amateur, is fraught with potential pitfalls. Your skills will need to be well used to distinguish between the many possible areas where you could advertise and to discover those where it is most effective to do so.

The techniques in this respect are very similar to those you already exercise in your selling, and relate to your ability to anticipate the reaction of your customer through your own empathy and understanding of him. You need to develop a gut feeling of how your advertising or promotion works before you accept that that is the right way to do it. However good the advertising display may be, it is useless if it is directed at the wrong audience, and it is a weak sales manager who believes that sort of decision should be left to the advertising department.

If, for example, you are an insurance salesman, you need to remember that you are selling peace of mind, not insurance. In addition, if you want to be most effective, you will ensure that you are selling a peace of mind which is unique to your own product, otherwise you are merely advertising a generic benefit which can be obtained, for example, through any insurance, not particularly the one that you are offering. As in selling, always advertise the benefit, not the product, and ensure that the benefit cannot be claimed also by others.

ADVERTISING: GOLDEN RULES

The guidelines for effective advertising are many. If you have an advertising division or agency, you should be wary how far you delegate the responsibility of how and where you advertise. Nevertheless, it is politic to recognise that advertising is a science and, while the opinions of how it should be done are always subjective and vary enormously, it is as well to make use of all the professional advice that you have available. You only have to look at the television commercials during one evening to see how you react to different presentations. You automatically reject some as unacceptable and regard others as totally successful, while another person, viewing the same advertising, will react quite differently. There are, however, some rules which you break at your peril.

Identify your audience

You must know who you are expecting to impress since without this information you cannot make a start. The person who will spend £100 insuring his car is probably not the same person who will spend £100,000 insuring his future. Each will read different papers, look at different hoardings and expect to see different advice when he does so. It will be your job to evaluate, through your marketing, who you are trying to contact.

Relate advertising cost to potential extra profit

You will need to make an accurate forecast of what you expect to achieve through your advertising and what additional profit you are looking to secure. Having done that, you can then decide how much of that expected profit it would be reasonable to spend on advertising or whether there might be a cheaper way of securing the same result.

Monitor the results

If at all possible, you will need to know, after the event, how successful the advertising has been. This is, in many industries, a difficult objective to fulfil and you may well have to accept that there is no real way you can attribute increased sales to increased advertising. Advertise a second-hand car in your local free newspaper and you can easily gauge the specific reaction that you get, the number of customers who showed interest and, indeed, at the end of the day whether or not you achieved your object in selling it. Advertise the facilities of a shop and you will never be sure whether those who come through the door come as a result of your advertising or might have come anyway.

Get the message across early

Whatever your method of advertising or promotion, make sure that the initial impact is secured in the first few seconds. The headline in display advertising is all-important and must, as far as possible, carry the full message. Remember that your readers may not get any further than that initial headline and you must get your message across as early as possible. As in selling, fail to get the customer's reaction in those first few moments, and his attention will drift elsewhere.

PAY-BACK CAN TAKE TIME

However, for all the rules which you will need to apply, never fall into the trap of letting others in your organisation decide that advertising is a precise science and can only be judged by the immediate results that you get. I worked at one time for a manufacturer of construction equipment who rejected all advertising simply because he was unable to quantify the results that each advertisement was securing. This was in spite of the fact that the lead time in purchasing was often up to one year and the equipment was capital plant costing many thousands of pounds. There is no way in that kind of business where advertising can possibly be quantified and yet advertising in the technical journals was effectively terminated by that company because the results could not be analysed. One has only to look at the phenomenal success of JCB throughout the world, and then to look at their marketing and advertising strategy which decided, many years ago, that they could take over the market, not by producing the best machines (which many of them are), but by ensuring that the machine which everyone thinks of, whether they are in the construction industry or not, bears their name.

EXHIBITIONS: A FORM OF ADVERTISING

Under the general heading of advertising I include also the proper use of exhibitions, since very many of the criteria applying to advertising inevitably apply also to exhibitions where a similar approach is made to encourage the customer to request further information about your product.

If the setting up of an exhibition becomes part of your responsibility, you will need to decide on a number of important aspects long before you get down to the detail of planning the exhibition itself. It is the decisions that you will take at this early stage that will influence how you plan the remainder and indeed how successful will be the final outcome. Basically, all your early considerations will come under the heading of the objective of exhibiting in the first place.

What market are you aiming for?

Are you launching a new product or service, or merely extending a market for your existing products? The first may call for more razzmatazz to get your message across, while the second will require a more conservative approach to re-present something of which your customers are probably already aware. The launch of a new car on the market is an example of the extent that a traditionally market orientated industry goes to get its message across in the most dramatic way possible, something it believes to be unnecessary as soon as the marque is established in the marketplace.

Who are you planning to convince?

What category of customer have you in mind? Obviously this will be an essential element in choosing your venue. The National Exhibition Centre in Birmingham will attract the commercial buyer who is prepared to visit an exhibition to look at all the available products. The market centre in Chipping Norton would be better placed for the double glazing company aiming to attract the casual shopper who might be induced to buy on impulse. Before you consider your venue, you must analyse the buying habits of those to whom you plan to sell.

How much can you afford to budget for the event?

There is little use spending more than you will earn and you will need to be well aware of the increased market share you are looking for. For example, you will need to know how many more items you must sell or how many more life policies you must sign to make the your exhibition stand viable. If you cannot make financial sense on paper beforehand, you are unlikely to do so on the day itself, and there is little point in regretting it all later when your analysis of the exhibition shows it all to have been a waste of time and money.

The necessity for professionalism

How professional must it all appear? It may well be that for the market in which you are working, the expertise of your own company (and yourself) is inadequate to secure a satisfactory result and that possibly a professional organiser is required. If so, it will cost money and if that expenditure is necessary, it had better be included early on in your budgeting. The argument that you cannot afford such luxuries is no argument at all for holding an exhibition which fails to impress simply because inadequate resources have been used to stage it. It would be better not to have held an exhibition at all. The cost of running any exhibition is high, but the final cost of running an ineffective one is a great deal higher.

Appoint a stand manager

Before the planning of your exhibition gets under way, ensure that at a very early stage you appoint a stand manager and that everyone knows who he is. It may, of course, be yourself, but think carefully before you take on that responsibility. You probably have enough to do already in your capacity as sales manager and a delegated stand manager should be able to take a great deal of the pre-planning and everyday organisation off your shoulders.

It will be the stand manager's job to ensure that the mechanics of the stand are properly set up, that contractors who are brought in are aware of what is expected of them and also complete their jobs satisfactorily. During the period of the exhibition, the stand manager will be responsible for the staffing and the ability of the personnel to handle the enquiries they are getting. He will closely watch whether the stand is undermanned or, indeed, overmanned. He will be responsible for ensuring that reports on visitors are completed and will take security control of those reports during the day. He will delegate the tidying of the stand both during and at the end of the day. He will also control the refreshments that are being offered, and should limit alcohol consumption both by uncontrolled stand staff and equally uncontrolled visitors.

Dealing with visitors

Guidance will need to be given to the stand staff, and the success of any exhibition will always be set by the standard of those responsible for meeting and dealing with the customers. Anyone in selling will be aware through professional videos and instruction books how not to behave at exhibitions, but, even so, at every exhibition you attend as a visitor, you will be greeted time and time again with the classic 'Can I help you?' – a question which will almost certainly generate the answer 'No, thank you'. It may well be that, having graduated to your new management position, you have personally got it right, but it is now going to fall on your shoulders to ensure that the personnel on your stand get it right as well. If you are going to manage and control exhibitions or displays where you meet the public, you will need, as a matter of urgency, to develop the skills of your stand staff to deal effectively with the potential customers who do arrive on your stand and not repel them before you have even found out what they wanted.

There are useful training films and videos available which will guide your personnel on effective exhibition behaviour, how to avoid the questions which generate a 'No' and how to develop the approach which encourages further conversation. Try to make use of these video presentations, remembering that very often you will have the facility in the hotel where accommodation for your staff has been arranged.

Your personnel should also be impressed with the importance of finding out early on who their visitors are, whether they have buying potential or whether they are time-wasters. If you have a time-waster on your hands, you may well be too polite to eject him immediately but at least you can gauge the amount of time you are prepared to give him.

Keep a record of all visitors

As sales manager, through your stand manager if you have one, it must be a major part of your job to ensure that all visitors and contacts are recorded, and that potential business customers are followed up swiftly in your subsequent sales operations. The stand manager may be responsible for the mechanics of this during the show, but, after the show is over, it is your own responsibility to use properly the information which has been gathered. I have had experience of many companies who do not have an adequate recording system and at the end of an exhibition really are not able to tell you, first, whether it was worth all the money and, secondly, whether the same exhibition should be scheduled for next year. Such managers will also be unable to tell you which of the stand staff were doing their job effectively and which were not. That is not the kind of managing which you are now being paid to do.

Debrief thoroughly

Lastly, after it is all over, if will be your job as sales manager to debrief everyone who has been concerned with the exhibition. This needs to be done while memories are still fresh and recorded so that it can be used as a base for your planning next year. If the catering was bad, record it so that you can change the company next year. If you had difficulty in booking convenient hotel accommodation, make sure that a note is made in the diary to finalise your arrangements earlier next time. Try to quantify the enquiries you have received. Euphoria is all very well, but it won't pay the bills of the exhibition you have just held, nor will it help you in persuading your finance director to let you have the same expenditure budget next year.

Exhibitions, small or large, may well be the only time that your sales force sit down and wait for the customers to arrive. If your exhibition is at a recognised centre, such as the Olympia or the National Exhibition Centre, it is often galling to be told afterwards. 'Yes, I visited the exhibition but I didn't get around to your stand'.

If, in your debriefing, you find that your customers got that close to you without any contact, then maybe you need to look closely at the magnetic power of your stand (or your salesmen) to discover why the customers didn't make that extra effort actually to visit you.

Exhibitions can be good selling or they can be bad selling. They can also be good, horrendously expensive selling. It is essential that you discover into which category your own operation falls so that you can remedy the errors which put you into the wrong category. 'Exhibitions are all a waste of time' is as stupid a generalisation as 'Meetings are all a waste of time', but the inefficient way that a great many exhibitions are organised and presented makes the generalisation more valid than it should be.

CHECKLIST

- Decide who your customers are before you use advertising to talk to them.
- Place your advertising with empathy. The publications you read may not be what your customers read.
- Budget carefully and do not spend more than your advertising will earn.
- Exhibitions are expensive and eat money. Treat the organisation of them casually and you will not see the money back.

13

Accurate forecasting of sales figures

'Business will either be better or worse.'
1872–1933, US president, Calvin Coolidge

FORECASTING: INFORMED ESTIMATING OR INSPIRED GUESSWORK?

Forecasting is probably one of the least attractive jobs that you have taken on as a sales manager. As a salesman, you will already have had experience of being asked to give your own estimates of future trends and prospects, and what you will now be asked to do is very similar, but on a larger scale. You will also have the added problem of being further from the action and from the factors which might influence the forecasts you will be putting forward. However, decisions will be made on the figures you produce and the skills you need to develop to get those figures as accurate as possible will play a great part in determining how successful a manager you are.

Forecasting, whether you like it or not, is an essential part of the job you have taken on. Unlike accountants, who have the somewhat easier job of telling you what you have sold, the sales or marketing manager must anticipate a wide range of variables, such as economic climate, interest rates, industrial growth and other factors, and apply them to another range of variables such as customer acceptance, competitive activity and future company sales achievement, and then produce a figure which can, with some confidence, be used in company forward planning. The result will, unless luck plays a major part in the result, often be wide of the mark that is actually achieved.

Unfortunately, the inspired guess, which is your other option, is equally likely to be inaccurate, but for all that it is imperative that an accurate forecast as possible is obtained, as a great amount of forward planning, both yours and of others, will have to be made based on the figures you have produced.

A BASIS FOR FORECASTING

You will need to look at forecasting in many different ways, but basically you will arrive at your figures by looking at two considerations. The first is derived from the past and requires you to assume that there will be no changes in the factors likely to affect what you are doing. From this you calculate figures for a similar period in the future. This is in principle a fairly easy mathematical analysis, as you have history to lean on and you are merely projecting past trends into the future. You were on a rising curve last year and there is no reason to think you will not continue it for the next one as well. However, it is when you follow this through with the second part of your analysis that the crystal ball becomes part of your equipment.

This, the second stage, assumes there will be changes and tries to work out with some accuracy what they will be, whether they are internal to your product or company (and so controllable) or external, in which case you have no alternative but to follow them. Either way, you then need to calculate the effect they will have on those basic estimates you originally forecast. In this you will need to use your powers of persuasion, as your directors may well see a rising sales curve as something that will automatically be expected to continue and may argue against the possibility of outside factors having any great influence on changing the situation. Remember that your forecast is not an ambition, but is a factual analysis of what is the most likely probability.

As a sales manager, you obviously need, for your own purposes, to have forecasts which enable you to set targets and gauge achievement, but there are many others who will use those same forecasts in their own forward planning.

Planning manufacturing or service costs

If you are manufacturing a product, or even developing a service, your production team (and I use the term in a somewhat general way) will need to have an accurate estimate, often well ahead, of their anticipated turnover and throughput, so that they can plan to have the proper facilities available to deal with it when it comes. Forecasting sales is not confined just to the factory where raw material requirements and completed stocks demand it. It is equally important in the service industries where promotional expenditure, expansion of the sales and administration team, and many other factors will all stem from the type of forecast that is made.

Planning manpower and promotional costs

If you are launching a new service, you will need to plan how many extra salesmen will be required to get it off the ground and, indeed, based on the profit you anticipate making, how many you can afford to employ. You will also need to know how much advertising the profit from the new venture can accommodate and how much risk you can take with that advertising before the profit is actually gained.

Requirements of a phased budget

If your forecast through the year is a variable one, changing month by month, you will need to be able to plan so that you have the resources each month to deal with it. It may be that the appointment of new sales staff to promote your product needs to be geared to the pace at which you plan to expand.

Briefing the financial team

Your financial team, who will be planning your cash flow, must have accurate guidance on the new demands that a new project, or the expansion of an existing one, will place on your funds. At the early stages of any project, you will probably find that you are spending more than you are making and it will save a great deal of subsequent recriminations if everyone is aware that the early loss you are making has been anticipated. Remember that many new ventures fail in midstream simply because the cash to promote them further is no longer available.

The figures which will trigger the right replies to all of these questions will be based on your own intuitive judgement and the way that the market is likely to act, or indeed how you can make it act and, while the accuracy of five-year or ten-year projected figures, popular ten years ago, now tend to be regarded with more suspicion, the immediate one-year or two-year figures are probably the ones on which planners will base their own projected schemes.

TAKING A BROADER VIEW OF THE FUTURE

It is, of course, always a gamble whether the initial figures you come up with are a solid foundation for the decisions which will follow, but the companies who fail to make such forecasts simply because they are as likely to be wrong as right are travelling blind into the future, when a little thought might just give them the edge over those who haven't thought it out at all. Your skill will involve anticipating events both in your company and also in the world outside. An ability, however unusual, to spot a recession before it happens would be of immense value in guiding your production and indeed your future employment plans, while a similar anticipation of a boom would enable your company to be well prepared for the business which is generated by it.

A number of crystal balls at your elbow will be of great assistance.

Inform yourself about your competitors

You will need to have your ear closely to the ground on the activities of your competitors. It is not an accident that industrial espionage is still a growth industry throughout the world. While I would not advocate the use of underhand methods to acquire your information, it is still essential that you get it somehow and do not proceed in ignorance of the activities of your closest competitors. It is certainly true that what *you* are doing will be of immense interest to *them*. If you are all manufacturing the same basic product as before, or offering the same basic service, then past performance might be a useful guide, but a revolutionary innovation or launch by yourselves (or your competitors) can well upset the whole balance of who gets what in the available market.

Your marketing research is vital

If you are launching a new product, your own marketing work on the viability of that product will initially be the best guide that you have on whether you will be able to take business which up to that time you have not been able to include in your plans. Marketing surveys and the like are, however, minefields with their own particular problems and one can list many products that failed to sell, after, one presumes, proper marketing operations. The Sinclair C5 powered bicycle was rejected by the buying market and was possibly carried to that market more by wishful thinking than by actual research, but it is not too difficult to imagine a positive response to questions asked of a buying public as to whether they would accept such a vehicle or not. It was mainly because of the bad publicity that the machine generated when it was actually launched that subsequent efforts to sell and promote it fell on deaf ears.

Study political developments

You must also be a dedicated student of politics. For example, a rise in the housing market can be anticipated so that it is not a surprise when it comes. New services and offers in the financial world will often be linked to changes in tax laws in relation to which such new propositions will be more attractive. The stated economic manifestos of particular political parties will often tell you well in advance what their future policies are likely to be. If you are in the field earlier than others, this might indicate an increase in the figures you are including in your forecast.

THE UPS AND DOWNS OF FORECASTING

There *are* employers who descend on subordinates who make an inaccurate forecast and unfairly blame them for all the inevitable results of that error. For that reason, and also because some people have difficulty in delegating, you will find many companies where forecasting is only ever done by board members and others often so far removed from the scene of operations that they really do not have the knowledge at their elbows to make forecasts at all. Like a weather forecaster, you will, of course, sometimes be wrong and if your employer does not realise you are dealing with an imprecise science, you have a problem on your hands. Even different experts in the same company will see the potential from a different aspect and produce a different set of figures for you to add to your own. Averaging all these options may well be an answer, but if you are going to carry the can for the figures, it is probably better that you rely on your own feeling of what is right or wrong and make your own decisions on how you see the situation.

You must know how wrong any forecast is likely to be, either overestimated or overestimated, so that you are always in a position to assess the risk you are taking by relying on that precise forecast in the first place, but always remember that forecasting your sales can be as unreliable as forecasting the football pools and decisions taken on the basis of that forecasting are equally at risk.

Even though there are many pitfalls, not the least being the assumption that what you did last year is a possible guide to what you will do next, it is still essential to base all your planning on as reliable an estimate as you can get. The wider the band of error, the higher the risk you are taking, while the narrower the band, the more certain you can be in the decisions you are going to take based on those figures.

Remember, however, that while your forecast figures are not your sales objective, that objective needs to be closely related to them. If you set targets to your sales force which are substantially higher than that forecast, you will be at risk on a number of counts. First, your salesmen may well consider that you are asking them to do the impossible and react accordingly, and remember that you will find it difficult to justify the figures you are asking of them, and secondly, if they do achieve those targets, the forecast which has also been used for the expansion of your administration will have created insufficient facilities to handle the business which arrives. It is far better, whatever your product or service, to work on the same set of figures both for forecasts and targets, so that all divisions are aware that they have the same object in view. They will, anyway, be your personal target since they are presumably what you consider sensible and are essentially what you can expect to happen, either if you continue the way you are going at present or alternatively if you introduce changes in your system.

Forecasting demands a contribution from everyone in your marketing and sales operation, and particularly from the field sales force who should know better than most what is likely to happen in the market. In the end, however, it will be very much down to you, as sales manager, to take all the figures you are given and then apply your own skills to produce the forecast calculations that everyone else will then work on. Unfortunately, if at the end of the year you are right, those who provided the original figures will probably claim the credit, while if you are wrong, there will not be many others stepping forward to take the blame.

CHECKLIST

- Any forecasting is likely to be wrong, but at least it has a better chance than an inspired guess.
- The past history is always helpful, but it must be adjusted to meet probable future influences.
- To be efficient, all divisions of your company should make use of your forecast figures. However, get it wrong and they will be wrong also.
- Know how wrong a forecast is likely to be and what risks you are taking by acting on it.

14

The skill of leading from the front

'Leadership is action, not position.'

Donald H McGannon

THE LEADER OF THE TEAM

I said at the beginning of this book that the job of management is to manage and whoever first made that observation understood what the whole principle of management was about. He also understood the main reason why managers often fail. They fail because they see their promotion as having the same job that they had before, but on a different scale and with more authority than they had previously. Management is not that and companies who want their managers to act in that way are not making proper use of the personnel they have employed.

A manager is there to set up his organisation, whether sales or otherwise, so that his company is in the right position to survive when problems arise. He is there to make decisions which, as a salesman in the past, he would never have made, and while he must also sell, that has now become a secondary part of his job.

His job, and, if you are reading this book, presumably yours also, is now to lead his salesmen from the front in a way that will give them the motivation and incentive to do things because they want to, not because they are being told to. Respect from subordinates is essential to gain this kind of support, and while instructions will often be carried out simply because those subordinates wish to keep their jobs, there will be little lasting effect unless everyone has the same confidence that the path they are following is the right one. You can get away with poor management, and can probably protect your own job at the same time, but in doing so you will fail to achieve the loyalty which will make your job easier and your sales force more efficient.

Remember that a manager who is mediocre for whatever reason, whether he has a chip on his shoulder, whether he lacks confidence in his own judgement or whether he simply has not got the skill to control, will eventually create a mediocre staff who have the same approach to the job that he has himself.

HOW DO YOU GET TO THE FRONT?

How, then, can you develop and recognise the talents that you need to ensure the respect of those who work for you? The following ideas will help you to decide how far down the road you are already and to take stock before you start your new job.

At the start, don't hurry

On taking up your new appointment, always wait before you evaluate your new employees and do not rely on first impressions, either to praise or criticise. When you are new is the one time you are able to change responsibilities and to make decisions, and if you do this too early before you have really analysed the operation, you will be wasting your moment. There will, in the first stages, be a rush by your employees to persuade you that each has more talent available than is at present being used. Bide your time before convincing yourself that the talent is really there.

Listen carefully

In the first few days or weeks, spend your time listening, not talking. There may well be time for a lot of talking later, but do it at the start and you may well later regret what you have said, and found you have taken decisions which were the wrong ones. As Peter Drucker says, 'My greatest strength as a consultant is to be ignorant and ask a few questions.'

Find out about people's jobs

You will need to be aware of the skills of your subordinates and what they need to do to carry out their jobs well. This does not necessarily mean that you must be personally capable of doing those jobs, although I would assume that you are unlikely to control salesmen unless you are already an experienced salesman yourself. Don't assume that your employees will expect you to know every detail about your new job and indeed about theirs. They will respect you if you ask for information, but will have little time for you if you don't ask and obviously need to. What is essential is that you should be well informed on what difficulties are involved in their jobs so that you are able to discuss their problems with them.

Put the past behind you

Make a firm resolution to forget your last company. What you did there is irrelevant (however good you thought it was). Constant references to how things 'used to be done' will do little to enhance your reputation. The ball-game is now solely in the present and in the future, and comparisons, either favourable or unfavourable, have no place in your new position.

Encourage salesmen to think and communicate

You must, as when you were a salesman, be ready to listen to what your subordinates tell you. They are, after all, paid for their skills and if you really believe that they have nothing to contribute to the sales operation, perhaps you should either not be employing them in the first place or at the very least be training them so that they *can* contribute. Good communication with your employees and interchangeability of ideas is also the only way to find out whether they are committed to you and the company or not.

Command respect, not fear

If you believe that fear has any place in your staff relationships, then you will receive the minimum co-operation that those staff can get away with. It is a style of management which is not uncommon and there are many disagreeable managers who, on the surface, appear to succeed, but they are doing it the hard way and they will find little loyalty to support them when things go wrong.

Debate salesmen's objectives

Do you discuss sales objectives with those who have to implement them or do you regard it as a matter of authority that such directions are your decision and not for discussion? If you do it the second way, you need not be surprised when your sales force rejects those objectives as being unreasonable.

Delegate decision making

Do you delegate decisions to those who have the skills to accept delegation or do you insist, because you have no confidence in them, that they report back before any decisions are taken? If you intend to take all the decisions yourself, simply because you believe it improves the chances of a good decision being made, you will gain little advantage by paying good salaries to employees who have experience and skills at their command.

Know your staff

Do you know all those who work for you? This includes not only the salesmen, but also the administrative staff and the person who makes the tea. It was Field Marshal Montgomery who said, 'It is difficult to be a leader of men if the men you lead do not know who you are.'

Surprisingly, it is not difficult to list out all the main reasons why managers fail in the job they are given. What is surprising is that with such a simple formula which guarantees success, so few managers in the field actually implement the rules which they know will give them that success. If you ask them why they do not follow the rules, they have the answer to that as well. They will tell you that, with the pressures of the job, they just did not have the time available and yet the reason why they did not have the time was simply because they were not planning and controlling their jobs in the way that would make the whole operation easier. Plan your own organisation with the following ideas in mind and you should secure more time to develop the control which is the trade mark of the efficient manager.

ANALYSE THE TEAM'S OBJECTIVE, THEN RECRUIT AND TRAIN THE TEAM

If you, as a manager, ensure that your staff are properly recruited and trained, many jobs which at present occupy your time can be competently handled by your employees. The argument that if you want something done well, you should do it yourself, is an admission that you have failed, for one reason or another, to set up your organisation in the way that it should be. It may even be true that, had you done the job yourself, it would have been done better, but if, in the process, you then neglect to carry out another function, possibly more important than the first, you are moving backwards rather than forwards.

If, because the workload or turnover has increased, you employ someone to assist you, then it is always pointless to continue with all the jobs for which you were previously responsible. It will certainly need changes in your own pattern and it will need confidence in the new man you have employed, but regular reallocation of those responsibilities is really what management in an expanding business is all about.

Of course your old customers will still want to deal with you rather than with your subordinates and there may be some way you will need to adapt to meet the needs of the more important customers, but do it as a general rule and you might as well not have appointed the subordinate in the first place. It may even be part of your job to persuade those customers that you now have a deputy who can act as effectively as you did, but persuade them you must if you are to have the time for your new responsibilities.

Many managers continue their careers as before, becoming super salesmen for their companies, and then wonder why they are removed when they are found to be unable to absorb their new duties. 'I was not given the time' is probably the most common remark as a manager leaves his office for the last time. His job was to make the time.

THE CAPTAIN HELPS THE TEAM PLAY

In your new duties, you will also need to spend a fair proportion of your time leading your staff so that the reasons why they give you their loyalty are the right ones. Remember that in the past you have had no need to demand loyalty, only give it, and you will, I am sure, recall how important it was as a salesman to have respect for the person you were working for and for the manner in which he led his sales force. If you did not have that respect, then your employment merely became a matter of money and you would always have been open to the highest bidder who might have encouraged you to move elsewhere. As a salesman, that might not necessarily have made you a less effective member of the team, but the manager who generates only a financial loyalty will have a continual problem with movement of staff and the additional hassle that it creates.

An enthusiastic team, moreover, will make decisions which will be taken without reference to you and, if they are motivated correctly, decisions which are in line with your own way of thinking. If, before any real decisions are made, your staff need to discuss the matter and then each time consult with you, then it is fairly evident that not only will important decisions be delayed, but you will also not have the time for the more responsible management duties which should be your job. I have met many sales managers who jealously retained all decisions on price, delivery, customer credit or whatever, on the basis that a wrong decision was their own responsibility and, in doing so, the skills of the subordinates, all of which were bought in at great expense, were never used. If you believe that centralised decision making is the only way to ensure the smooth running of your company, then you are possibly employing the wrong people as your subordinates.

WORK AT MOTIVATION

In the control and motivation of your staff, you should ask yourself whether you offer the same contact and discussion which motivated you when you were a salesman. Many salesmen will tell you that there have been times when management failed to recognise their contribution to their company's success and yet the moment that those same salesmen become managers, they often forget that their subordinates now need that same recognition. 'I do not have the time to have a personal relationship with all my salesmen' is the reply of a person who has been unable to set up a delegated organisation which gives him that time.

CONTROL THE PAPERWORK

The last obvious failing of almost every poor sales manager is an inability to emerge from the administrative mounds of paper which now surround him and to which, in the past, he as a salesman contributed his own share. Some of these bits of paper are, of course, awaiting decisions which others could make and it will only be when you delegate decisions that the bits of paper (and their successors) will disappear also. Some bits of paper will be unnecessary statistics, which, over the years, and in a system possibly created by your predecessor, will have been delivered week by week and are rarely read except when a once-yearly board meeting demands it. Find out if the board meeting actually requires such an expensively collected set of figures and, if not, delete it. Some will be part of a sales control system which may, or may not, be giving you the information you require. If, as is likely, the system was designed to meet the demands of a manager of two or three years ago, it may well not meet your own. Redesign it so that it tells you what you need and nothing more. As with many of these problems you will probably find that your sales administrator or office manager has the skill to filter what is useful and what is not, and has the authority to make a decision without your requiring to see the bit of paper at all. Remember that if the information you have discarded is later found to be indispensable, then it is easy enough to bring it back into the system.

It is your job to manage. It is not your job to be the office manager and it is certainly not your job to be a sales administrator. You need to spend your time at the sharp end which is where your sales force is and the argument that you have to spend most of your time in the office simply because there is a great deal there to do, essentially means that you have failed to control what there is to do. Fail to delegate, fail to filter (or have filtered for you) the important from the unimportant, spend your time as an office manager instead of a sales manager and you may soon find that an office manager is what you have become.

CHECKLIST

- You are no longer a salesman. A sales manager is a manager, not a super salesman.
- Mediocre management results in mediocre salesmen.
- Make yourself aware of what your sales team are individually capable of, and aim to use those talents by encouragement and promotion.
- Delegate to allow time to manage. Train others so that in time you can delegate further.
- Do not surround yourself with unnecessary administrative facts and figures.